ABOUT THE AUTHORS

SIMON CONSTABLE is host of the *News Hub* live web show, which airs weekdays at 4:00 p.m. ET on the Wall Street Journal Digital Network. He also makes stand-alone videos for WSJ.com, MarketWatch, and Barrons.com. He has written for *The Wall Street Journal*, WSJ.com, Dow Jones Newswires, MarketWatch.com, TheStreet.com, the *New York Post*, the *New York Sun*, and the *South China Morning Post*. He is also a frequent guest on Fox News, BBC, and ABC TV; a fill-in host for the *John Batchelor Show* on WABC Radio; and was previously a senior correspondent for TheStreet.com TV.

Constable holds an MBA from the Darden School of Business at the University of Virginia. He also worked on Wall Street as an adviser to top management at some of America's most prestigious companies. He lives in New York City.

ROBERT E. WRIGHT (PhD in History from the State University of New York–Buffalo, 1997) is the Nef Family Chair of Political Economy and the Director of the Thomas Willing Institute for the Study of Financial Markets, Institutions, and Regulations at Augustana College in Sioux Falls, South Dakota. He has authored or coauthored fourteen books with leading university presses and commercial publishers. He has also written for *Barron's*, the *Chronicle of Higher Education*, the *Los Angeles Times*, *McKinsey Quarterly*, and other prominent publications and has appeared on NPR, C-SPAN, Fox News, the BBC, BNN, MSNBC, various local TV news stations, and a dozen nationally syndicated radio programs. Wright also sits on the editorial board of the Museum of American Finance's *Financial History* magazine.

THE WALL STREET JOURNAL GUIDE TO

The 50 Economic Indicators

That Really Matter

THE WALL STREET JOURNAL GUIDE TO

The 50 Economic Indicators

That Really Matter

From Big Macs to "Zombie Banks," the Indicators

Smart Investors Watch to Beat the Market

SIMON CONSTABLE

and

ROBERT E. WRIGHT

HARPER
BUSINESS

HARPER
BUSINESS

The Wall Street Journal® is a registered trademark of Dow Jones and is used by permission of Dow Jones.

This book is written as a source of information only, and the information contained in it should not be considered a substitute for the advice, decisions, or judgment of the reader's professional advisers. Each investor's situation is different, and readers are encouraged to seek professional advice before making any investment decisions.

Illustrations throughout this book are used courtesy of *The Wall Street Journal.*

HarperCollins books may be purchased for educational, business, or sales promotional use. For information please write: Special Markets Department, HarperCollins Publishers, 10 East 53rd Street, New York, NY 10022.

FIRST EDITION

Library of Congress Cataloging-in-Publication Data

Constable, Simon, 1968–
    The Wall Street Journal guide to the 50 economic indicators that really matter : from Big Macs to "zombie banks," the indicators smart investors watch to beat the market / by Simon Constable and Robert E. Wright.—1st ed.
      p. cm.
Includes bibliographical references.
    ISBN-13: 978-0-06-200138-2 (pbk.)
    ISBN-10: 0-06-200138-8 (pbk.)
    1. Portfolio management. 2. Economic indicators. 3. Business forecasting.
I. Wright, Robert E. (Robert Eric), 1969- II. Title. III. Title: Guide to the 50 economic indicators that really matter.
HG4529.5.C658   2011
339.3—dc22

2010052579

---

11 12 13 14 15   OV/RRD   10 9 8 7 6 5 4 3 2 1

CONTENTS

Contents

GOVERNMENT (G)

NET EXPORTS (NX)

MULTIPLE COMPONENTS

Contents

INFLATION, FEAR, AND UNCERTAINTY

Contents

INTRODUCTION

T HIS BOOK IS ABOUT economic indicators. It must be—it says so on the cover! But it's more than that. It's about helping you protect your money. No matter how much or how little that is, you deserve to keep it and, with a little luck and a lot of savvy, see it grow. The best way to do that, we think, is to watch trends in data. Not just a few key metrics followed by everyone (yes, those too) but a whole slew of them, many of which most people have never heard of. We think to really have an edge, investors need to get creative, maybe even a little wacky, and look at the economy not just outside the box but inside the diner, the fast-food restaurant, and out on the street. You'll see what we mean by that later on, near the end of the book.

Anyone with any investment portfolio whatsoever knew pain when the Great Credit Crunch hurled stock markets into turmoil in 2008 and into 2009. Investors large and small watched while their wealth shrank by the day, and sometimes even by the hour.

This book is about you not letting that happen again. To achieve that we'll show you how the economic indicators we've chosen can help you see the turns in the economy before they happen. With that prescience you can then make changes to your investments ahead of time and avoid the suffering you probably felt during the past couple of years.

Protecting one's nest egg in this way is crucial to investing success. After all, what is the sense of beating the market for five, ten, or twenty years only to have the market beat you senseless in a financial crash? And after the ugliness is over, will you have the foresight and the guts to jump back in while the getting is still good? The financial crisis of 2008–9 and its aftermath suggest that most investors were insufficiently nimble because they were looking at what the economy was rather than what it would become.

While collectively these investors lost trillions of dollars, the problem is that many appear to be no wiser about the economy or investing than they were before the crisis. They seem destined to play it too safe when they should be making risky trades, and making risky investments when they should be playing it safe. In essence they will buy high then sell low, and then eventually buy back high again. That is the exact opposite of a profitable investment strategy.

Such an unhappy outlook for investors will remain the same—unless, that is, they digest the lessons of this book, which aims to teach investors how to invest across the business cycle, not just when prices are rising. In other words, this book intends to provide investors with sophisticated ways of thinking about the economy, not to lead them by the nose to specific investments. You know the parable about how giving a man a fish only feeds him for a day, but teaching him how to fish feeds him for a lifetime? The same goes for investing.

Use the Clues

Discerning the economy's direction—whether it will soar, plummet, or stagnate—may sound difficult, and it certainly isn't easy, but the economy can't help but constantly provide statistical clues about its health. Those clues can be seen using economic indicators. Some, called leading indicators, point to where the economy is heading. Others, called coincident, provide clues about its current position. Yet others, so-called lagging indicators, tell us where the economy has been. Leading indicators provide the most obvious basis for profit-making ideas, but concurrent and lagging indicators are important, too.

In case you haven't sensed it yet, at the points at which we discuss specific investment strategies and not just simple economics, we think mostly about intermediate and long-term investing, not day trading, foreign exchange dealing, derivatives swapping, or other forms of short-term speculation. That sort of stuff is best left to technical analysts, computers, and large sophisticated players.

Who we can help are people who want to use economic data and indicators to discern what is actually going to happen to the economy next month or next year and invest accordingly now to reap gains later.

If you look around enough bookstores, you're bound to encounter other books on economic indicators, including one that purports to unlock their secret clues and at least one that explicitly aims to help people with below-average intelligence understand some of the most complex concepts known to humanity.

We make neither claim. This book is certainly not for novices, but at the same time you don't have to already have a PhD in economics to understand it. It also contains no "secrets."

The information contained in this book, though often obscure to some people, is mostly readily available. All we have done is to find, compile, and explain it in what we hope readers will find a succinct and entertaining way.

We also believe that people have to do at least some research and forecasting on their own. A wet-behind-the-ears beginner can't tell the difference between a true expert, a quack, and a knave. So it is important to develop some expertise of your own.

The Fantastic 50

When we decided to put together a list of indicators to help readers understand what was going on in the economy we wanted to develop one that covered the entire economy. We also decided to exclude some of the big indicators that you've likely heard of. So you won't find the CPI (the Consumer Price Index measure of price inflation) in our list because even those with just a casual interest in the economy have heard of that common measure of inflation. Knowing what everyone else knows will not put you ahead of the pack.

Instead you need to look beyond the obvious. That's why

our list is mostly well off the beaten track. The indicators included can help you understand where inflation (and not just consumer prices), GDP (gross domestic product, the measure of the entire output of goods and services in the economy), and (un)employment are going next—but before they go there.

If fifty sounds daunting, keep in mind that the economy is a shape-shifting beast best examined from many angles and multiple perspectives. Some perspectives are more important than others, but all help to provide a more nuanced and textured portrait of the business cycle. And you really do need a sophisticated portrait of the economy because there is no one-size-fits-all indicator.

Many indicators move wildly up and down from month to month for random reasons, such as a freak storm or a fluke order. Moreover, due to pressure to put numbers out quickly, many indicators are merely guesstimates that will be revised later, sometimes drastically. Finally, many indicators, like house sales, have to be seasonally adjusted. Adjustment techniques, however, are far from foolproof and may over- or undercompensate for seasonal fluctuations.

Analyzing a selection of carefully chosen indicators is a better way of sorting out what's known as "statistical noise." The intuition behind our view that many indicators should be consulted is simple: the more indicators that point in the same direction, the more likely they are pointing to a real economic phenomenon and not a random or seasonal change. We consider the indicators we chose to be the best based on four simple criteria:

1. Timeliness: If the information is stale before it is available, why bother?

2. Accuracy: If the data is unreliable or is frequently revised, why bother?

3. Exoticness: If most investors already know and use it, why bother?

4. Degree of linkage to the real economy or the practical world of investing: If it doesn't tell us where things are going, where the economy is now, or where it has been, why bother?

Having spent a combined period of over half a century engrossed in economics and economic history, we had a good sense of where to start. But that alone wasn't enough. Like anyone else we are prone to human error. So we asked colleagues—journalists, financial market professionals, and academics—to see what they thought of our list. We took note of their comments and made the necessary modifications. We are grateful for the input.

One thing we note about our selection process: Even among the people we know—people who spend all day, every day, thinking about economics and investing—no one was previously aware of every one of the Fantastic 50. That's right. It seemed there was a surprise for everyone—a Christmas come early for economists if you like.

In short, if you want to know where the economy has been, where it is, and where it is headed, start here!

How This Book Works

We describe our Fantastic 50 in a standardized four-part format. Section 1 provides a short description and section 2 a time series graph or other illustration. Section 3 is called "Investment Strategy" and provides tips on how to use the indicator. Finally, section 4 briefly summarizes the indicator's key aspects and provides a short discussion of where to get the data.

The most famous equation in physics is Einstein's $E=MC^2$. The equivalent for macroeconomics is GDP = C + I + G + NX. This equation represents the components of GDP, the most widely accepted measure of economic activity in the economy. More plainly, it tells us how much stuff the economy produced in a given quarter or year.

With that equation in mind we arranged our indicators alphabetically within those broad categories of consumption (C), business investment (I),[1] government (G), and net exports (NX). Those components encompass everything that happens in an economy, and we have indicators for each one.

We also put together an additional category for indicators that point simultaneously to multiple GDP components. On top of that we included a final category for indicators that point

---

[1] Readers should not confuse "investment" with "business investment." Business investment involves buying new machinery or building new factories. In some contexts, investments are any sums of money invested in financial or other assets in the hope of economic gain. Buying equities in a secondary market is an example of financial investment not business investment, for example, because it does not represent new net investment in the economy, just a change of owners. Throughout the book, we will try to clearly differentiate between the type of investment that readers might make from the business investment (I) used by economists in GDP calculations.

to inflation, fear, and/or uncertainty. While this way of organizing the material will be intuitive to anyone who has taken basic courses in economics, it also means that the book begins with some of the more technical indicators. Those interested in the sexier chapters should not fret, however, as the ending is spicier and can be skipped to at any time with a few flicks of the thumb and forefinger or clicks on the computer keyboard. The Fantastic 50 is not a linear narrative that must be encountered page by page but rather a web that can be explored at will.

As part of our research for each indicator, we interviewed seasoned professionals who are intimate with how different statistics reflect changes in the underlying economy. You will find quotes and explanations from them to give you the benefit of their wisdom and to help give you a three-dimensional, textured view of the economy in general and investing in particular. As you will see, we cast our net wide in this endeavor.

We have also embedded our Fantastic 50 with a few helpful "apps." For faster reference, each indicator is clearly labeled as leading, coincident, lagging, or some combination thereof. Cross-references to related or similar indicators are prominently displayed too. Finally, at the end of each indicator you'll find an "Exec Summary" box that concisely reviews seven of its most important attributes:

- **When to look for the data.**

- **Where to look for the data.**

- **What to watch for in the data.**

- **What that means in terms of the outlook for the economy or a particular sector.**

- **What to do to make yourself some money or to prevent yourself from losing some:** Some of the advice is very specific, like what investment decisions to make under what circumstances. Some of it is more generic. In the simplest terms, make safer investments when the economy is going into a recession and riskier ones when it is coming out of a slump. We've also added a more technical note at the bottom of this page to help explain other aspects further. [2]

- **Risk level of the investment strategy suggested above.**

- **Profit potential of assuming the risks described above, where each $ represents up to 10% annual return:** Risk and reward are of course positively correlated—the higher

---

[2] If you think nominal interest rates are headed downward—as they typically move during a recession—buy bonds, because they will increase in price. (Nominal interest rates and bond prices are inversely related. If you didn't know that or otherwise feel that your basic background is a little shaky, read Wright and Quadrini's *Money and Banking* textbook first. It's free at www.flatworldknowledge.com/printed-book/1634. Also available free, on the Thomas Willing Institute's website, www.augie.edu/thomaswilling, is an extensive glossary of financial terms.) If you think nominal interest rates are headed upward due to an economic expansion or because inflation is headed skyward, short (most simply sell, or borrow some bonds, sell them high, and buy more of them back at lower prices, as described in the short interest entry below) bonds, because they will be hit hard. Use the new cash to buy gold, real estate, and other assets expected to appreciate in line with (or better yet, faster than) the prices of other goods. If the economy looks to heat up without inflationary pressures, pro-cyclical stocks in the financial, industrial, and construction sectors are a good bet. When recession looms, by contrast, defensive stocks like food and utilities are probably the way to go. And if panic or crisis appears imminent, Treasuries will likely soar, just as they did in September 2008.

the risk assumed, the higher the potential reward. Please note we used the word "potential" in the previous sentence. The higher the possible payoff, the less likely it becomes. But you knew that (we hope!).

Is it really necessary to learn about and track all fifty of these indicators in order to thrive as an investor? No, you could get really, really lucky and stumble onto the next Google, a tech stock that made early investors rich. Of course you are just as likely to buy the next Enron or Lehman Brothers—both now-defunct firms that were once big players in financial markets. In simple terms, the more data you track the better an intuitive feel you will have for what is really going on in the economy. At first it may seem confusing or you may feel you are learning less and less. But pretty soon you'll start seeing the big picture and that will help you invest better.

You're human, so you'll still make mistakes that will cost you money. However, if you use the knowledge contained in this book, such losses will likely be smaller and more quickly reversed. Additionally, if you learn to listen to the economy's rhythms you can pick appropriate asset sectors before most other investors, giving you a distinct advantage. The indicators explained in the following pages will help you to maximize exposure in the right places and minimize it in the wrong ones, so read on and never stop studying.

CONSUMPTION

(C)

THIS SECTION DETAILS FIVE indicators of consumption, a category that includes personal expenditures on durable goods such as cars, furniture, and appliances; nondurable goods such as food, clothing, and fuel; and services such as health care, transportation, education, and recreation.

These days, consumption constitutes about 70% of the U.S. economy, making it a category you can't ignore. Monitoring the indicators in this section of the book will keep your finger on the pulse of this huge component of economic activity.

1

AUTOMOBILE SALES
Leading into Recessions,
Coincident with Lagging Recoveries

(*See also* ISM Manufacturing Survey)

Back in 1953 the head of GM, Charles Wilson, said that "what was good for the country was good for General Motors and vice versa." It's still true that cars (GM's or otherwise) count when it comes to the economy, especially for the manufacturing sector.

Just think about all the things that are needed to make a car or truck: steel sheet for body panels, paint, glass for windshields and lights, copper for electrical wiring, rubber for tires, plastic, fabric, and possibly leather for interiors. What it all means is that when the big car companies like Ford Motor, Toyota, General Motors, Chrysler, Honda, and Hyundai are making and selling cars, then businesses in a lot of ancillary industries are working hard too.

"This is not a niche indicator," says Campbell Harvey,

professor of finance at Duke University's Fuqua School of Business. "The auto industry is interconnected with so much else that by watching its movements you get some view of the overall health of the economy."

For most people, the cost of a car or truck is large—a major purchase second only to the cost of buying a house or apartment. A new car that costs thirty thousand dollars (not an unreasonable price at the time of writing in 2010) would be a large chunk of many folks' pretax annual income, and greater than a year's pay for some. As a result, many people borrow money to buy cars and trucks. When they do, it tells us something about how confident they feel about their economic and financial future. "They are not going to go out and buy a car if they think there is reasonable chance they'll get laid off," explains Harvey.

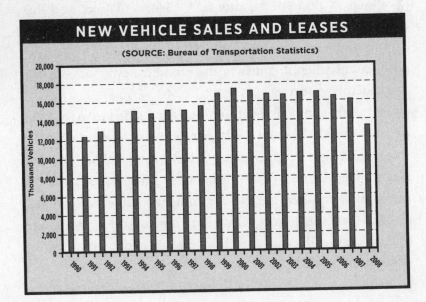

NEW VEHICLE SALES AND LEASES
(SOURCE: Bureau of Transportation Statistics)

Investment Strategy

Car sales are a decent leading indicator of impending recessions as people tend to back off buying cars when they don't feel confident about their jobs. Coming out of a recession, car sales tend to lag because most people wait until the economy has clearly turned upward before making such a major purchase.

As shown in the accompanying chart, sales of new autos slowed before the 2000–1 downturn. They picked up a little during the mid-decade boom before dropping dramatically in 2007 as the economy began to show signs of weakness.

One of the keys with automobile sales is to focus on sales and leases of new cars because, in the end, they drive the other parts of the economy. The sale of a used car doesn't actually mean any new materials were used, although it's still a good sign that people want to buy another vehicle.

That said, when parsing the automobile sales data you need to look for trends.

"Try to detect a clear momentum, a positive or negative trend," says Harvey. "Take a look at where we are relative to recent history and see if there is any consistency."

If there is a consistent decrease in sales, then we are likely seeing the economy head into a period of weakness, he says. Likewise, if the trend is higher, then the economy may be improving. Harvey also notes that the fact that so many people borrow to buy cars can actually disturb the sales trends a bit. During economic slowdowns interest rates tend to fall, thus making borrowers' car payments much lower, sometimes dramatically so. That added affordability can sometimes drive sales up a tad better than expected when the economy is weak.

When automobile sales look like they are signaling a slowdown or recession, it makes sense to avoid investing in assets usually sensitive to the economic cycle. In other words, shun stocks in favor of government securities and high-quality corporate bonds.

EXEC SUMMARY: AUTOMOBILE SALES

When to look: Auto sales figures are released on the first business day of each month. The data covers the previous month's sales.

Where to look: Reporters working for *The Wall Street Journal* file breaking news stories on WSJ.com as the various auto companies release their data. When all the data is released, an overall story is published that explains all the figures and interprets the state of the industry.

Go to *The Wall Street Journal* online's, "Market Data Center" for a quick read of the data and how it compares to what investors were expecting. You'll find the data center at www.WSJMarkets.com. When you are there, you'll need to go to the "Calendars & Economy" section and find the "Auto Sales" link.

Other sources include the website of the Bureau for Transportation Statistics: www.bts.gov/publications/national_transportation_statistics/. The car-making companies, such as General Motors, Ford Motor, Chrysler, Hyundai, Honda, and Toyota, also provide detailed disclosures of their sales figures.

What to watch for: Decreases in new automobile sales and leases.

What it means: People are pulling back due to fears about their future employment status.

What to do: Avoid investing in assets usually sensitive to the economic cycle. In other words, shun stocks in favor of government securities and high-quality corporate bonds.

Risk level: Medium.

Profit possibility: $$

2

CHAIN STORE SALES
Coincident

A MERICANS LOVE TO CONSUME stuff, and consumption is a vital part of our overall economic well-being. Because most of us go to retailers in order to buy goods and services, we can gain insights into the health of consumption by looking at retail sales.

Although much of the data on the retail sector is available only long after the fact, some of it is very timely, and it comes from some of the most sophisticated retailers in the world, including chain stores like Saks (SKS) and The Gap (GPS) and membership warehouse retail stores such as BJ's (BJ) and Costco (COST). Together, the chain stores represent only 10% of overall retail sales, but the data about these companies' sales is available every Tuesday for the week through the prior Saturday.

This data is important for more than just its timeliness. Chain stores tend to operate across the entire United States and not just regionally. So we can get a national read on the state of consumption.

In addition, chain stores are master sellers. They use the latest selling techniques and hire the savviest marketers. They also have the financial weight and the robust distribution systems to get first dibs on the latest new gadgets. Why does this matter? Because if the big guys aren't selling, then the rest of the retail world stands little chance.

There are two sources of basic data: the Johnson Redbook *Index* and the ICSC-Goldman Sachs Weekly U.S. Retail Chain Store Sales Index. Both entities also put out monthly figures. (For a broader view that includes smaller retailers as well, see the Census Bureau's monthly retail sales report.)

Investment Strategy

Economic forecasters should watch this data closely because of the giant portion of overall GDP that consumption represents. When the data shows that chain store sales have increased, then the consumption component of the overall economy is probably doing quite well. When chain store sales are weak or falling, then the opposite is likely true.

Data on chain store sales can also be used when deciding whether to invest in retail stocks like Saks (SKS), Target (TGT), and J.Crew (JCG).

But you need to be careful. "You have to be really good and nimble to buy a stock based on this data," says Kristin Bentz, a veteran retail industry analyst at the Conshohocken, Pennsylvania–based investment bank PMG Capital.

JOHNSON REDBOOK INDEX: SELECTED DATA

Date	Redbook Index YoY%	Retailer Target YoY%	Sales Base $bin	MoM Change* %	Target %	Retail Month #wks	Retail Month End
Jul-07	2.89	2.8	17.53	0.12	0.0	4	08/04/07
Aug-07	2.39	2.0	17.56	-0.32	-0.7	4	09/01/07
Sep-07	1.99	2.6	17.83	1.17	1.7	5	10/06/07
Oct-07	2.10	2.3	17.73	-0.45	-0.2	4	11/03/07
Nov-07	2.39	2.3	17.65	-0.16	-0.2	4	12/01/07
Dec-07	1.32	1.2	17.80	-0.21	-0.3	5	01/05/08
Jan-08	0.54	1.1	18.07	-5.64	1.3	4	02/02/08
Feb-08	0.48	0.7	17.66	-2.33	-2.1	4	03/01/08
Mar-08	1.06	1.4	17.84	1.60	2.0	5	04/05/08
Apr-08	1.60	1.8	17.50	-1.42	-1.3	4	05/03/08
May-08	1.82	1.7	17.54	0.47	0.4	4	05/31/08
Jun-08	2.59	2.8	17.26	-0.86	-0.7	5	07/05/08
Jul-08	2.92	2.9	17.43	1.31	1.3	4	08/02/08
Aug-08	1.74	1.6	17.43	-1.14	-1.3	4	08/30/08
Sep-08	1.25	1.7	17.31	-1.13	-0.7	5	10/04/08
Oct-08	0.57	0.7	17.36	-0.42	-0.3	4	11/01/08
Nov-08	-0.91	-0.5	17.41	-1.16	-0.7	4	11/29/08
Dec-08	-0.95	0.6	17.30	-0.68	0.8	5	01/03/09
Jan-09	-2.30	-1.8	17.10	-2.68	-2.0	4	01/31/09
Feb-09	-1.62	-1.9	17.04	0.76	0.4	4	02/28/09
Mar-09	-0.80	-0.8	16.92	0.09	0.1	5	04/04/09
Apr-09	0.49	0.3	16.93	1.37	1.1	4	05/02/09
May-09	-0.09	0.2	16.97	-0.34	-0.1	4	05/30/09
Jun-09	-4.38	-4.2	16.96	-4.34	-4.1	5	07/04/09
Jul-09	-5.64	-5.0	16.91	-1.62	-0.9	4	08/01/09
Aug-09			16.58			4	08/29/09

* Month-to-month changes are seasonally adjusted. For the current month, the Johnson Redbook Index is the month-to-date average until the month is closed.

** As of June, 2009, Walmart is no longer included in our retail sample.

Still, she has some useful tips for the would-be investor. In the first place, not all of the chain store sales data is that useful to investors. Sales of big retailers go up and down for many reasons including the opening and closing of different stores. To get useful information, new stores (those open less than twelve months) need to be excluded.

Instead, investors in retail companies look at the sales of stores open for a year or more. The data is known as the same-store sales in the United States and (like-for-like sales in Britain). It's a measure of the efficiency of retailing operations. This data is available the first Thursday every month, so it's not as timely as the raw data but it's far more useful for investors.

"When picking a stock to buy you want sequential and year-over-year same-store-sales growth," Bentz says. More simply: The data should show increased sales when compared to the same period a year ago and when compared to the prior month.

"That tells you the product is right, the trend is right, and the customers are coming back month after month," she explains.

On top of that it's important to look at what expectations of same-store sales were for that period. A company can have the right year-on-year and sequential results but still fall short of what analysts were expecting, and in that case the stock would likely suffer.

"When you get sequential and period growth, and the company is beating forecasts, then that's a buy," notes Bentz.

She adds that during the boom years it made some sense to look at exchange-traded funds that tracked the value of a basket of retail stocks, like the SPDR S&P Retail (XRT) ETF. But during the Great Recession things changed. Now, she says, not all retailers are created equal and it therefore makes sense to pick and choose which stocks to buy.

EXEC SUMMARY: CHAIN STORE SALES

When to look: For monthly same-store-sales data, be on watch the first Thursday of the month; weekly data from ICSC and Redbook data are available early Tuesday mornings.

Where to look: *The Wall Street Journal* closely follows retail sales figures. *Journal* reporters file breaking news reports on retail sales figures as the numbers are released. Check for articles covering the entire industry, as well as those with company-by-company detail.

Go to *The Wall Street Journal* online's "Market Data Center" for a quick read of the data and how it compares to what investors were expecting. You'll find the data center at www.WSJMarkets.com. When you are there, you'll need to go to the "Calendars & Economy" section, look for "U.S. Economic Events," and find the links to ICSC and Redbook on Tuesdays. Monthly same-store-sales data is available directly on many publicly traded retailers' websites.

The Johnson Redbook Index is available to clients of Redbook Research, although there are some samples available at no charge on its website: www.redbookresearch.com.

For those willing to pay, Bentz recommends going to Retail Metrics, where proprietor Ken Perkins provides an "enormous" spreadsheet of all the data.

What to watch for: Increases (declines) in year-over-year same-store-sales growth, as well as month-to-month increases.

What it means: Stores are doing well (struggling).

What steps to take: Buy (sell) as expectations of year-over-year same-store sales improve (degrade).

Risk level: Medium.

Profit possibility: $$

3

CONSUMER SENTIMENT
Leading

THE UNITED STATES MAY be many things, but if nothing else it is a nation of spenders. As a result, investors and economists devote a massive amount of time worrying what "the consumer" thinks, or how he is feeling. Simply speaking, when consumers feel better they spend more.

Despite all that angst, very few economic indicators just plain ask the proverbial man on the street, "How are you feeling?" Most other indicators measure what people have done or are doing.

The simple idea of asking what you and I are thinking or feeling has been taken up by two institutions: The Conference Board and the University of Michigan, which publish the Consumer Confidence Index (CCI) and the Michigan Consumer Sentiment Index (Michigan Sentiment), respectively.

These two indices pretty much measure the same thing: How good are you feeling, economically speaking, right now and how do you feel about the future? The data is collected by polling households.

Simply speaking, higher numbers on these indicators indicate that consumers believe the economy will improve or that it will continue to chug along. For instance, if the CCI increases from 49 in April to 55 in May, consumers believe that conditions are improving. Likewise a lower or falling number does not augur well for the future of the economy.

The Michigan Sentiment survey is published twice each month, with the first reading out slightly ahead of the CCI. In addition, the Michigan Sentiment is included in other government statistics, which gives it added weight with observers.

But for those willing to dig beyond the headline figures, the CCI is useful also. It includes survey data on spending plans for big-ticket items such as cars and major appliances. There is also data on inflation expectations and a breakdown of sentiment by age and income.

A minor problem with both of these indices: They are very volatile, and there is frequently so much noise, so many random ups and downs in the results that it makes them hard to interpret.

Part of the reason for this volatility is that the psyche of the individual being polled can be affected by many things. For instance, a spike in gasoline prices or terrorist attacks can weigh down on consumer sentiment. The chart of University of Michigan's index visually illustrates the short-run volatility. But it also shows that sentiment generally falls dramatically going into recessions.

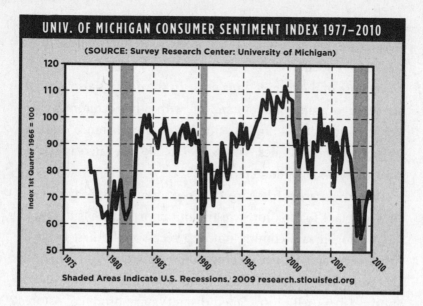

UNIV. OF MICHIGAN CONSUMER SENTIMENT INDEX 1977–2010

(SOURCE: Survey Research Center: University of Michigan)

Index 1st Quarter 1966 = 100

Shaded Areas Indicate U.S. Recessions. 2009 research.stlouisfed.org

Investment Strategy

Because of the huge volatility in the two sentiment indicators, investors need to proceed with caution when using them. "What we really try to do is look at the trend, not a single point in time," says Art Hogan, chief market analyst at investment banking firm Jefferies in New York. Or more simply, one sunny data point does not signal an economic summer. A jump in sentiment could occur for any number of reasons that don't reflect a sustainable trend. "Try to blend out that one-month figure and look at a three-month moving average and that will make a wiser investment decision," Hogan says.

Sometimes, as in 1980 and 2001, the index accurately reflects dips in the market. However, during the 1981–82, 1990, and 2008–9 recessions, by contrast, consumer confidence increased and fell back once, twice, even three times before those recessions ended.

Because of the tremendous noise in the data it's also good to use these indicators in conjunction with other economic clues like the indicators found in this book. For instance, look at consumer durable sales or whether banks are increasing the availability of consumer credit.

When you are fairly sure that sentiment is improving, the obvious place to look for investment opportunities is the retail sector. Hogan says coming out of a recession he first looks at consumer-staple stocks—stores like Walmart (WMT) that sell necessities like basic foodstuffs and sundries. He then moves on to retailers selling so-called discretionary products—stores like Coach (COH) and Tiffany & Co. (TIF)—that sell products, often luxuries, that don't absolutely *need* to be purchased.

Likewise, when it looks like the economy is headed south, investors should take the reverse tack and get out of the luxury names first.

EXEC SUMMARY: CONSUMER SENTIMENT

When to look: At 10 a.m. ET, on the last Tuesday of the month, look for Conference Board Consumer Confidence data. For the initial reading of the Michigan Sentiment information, be alert on the second Friday of the month.

Where to look: *The Wall Street Journal* closely follows consumer sentiment survey data. *Journal* reporters file breaking news reports on these metrics as the information is released by the different organizations. Go to *The Wall Street Journal* online's "Market Data Center" for a quick read of the data and how it compares to what investors were expecting.

You'll find the data center at www.WSJMarkets.com. When you are there, you'll need to go to the "Calendars & Economy" section. Look for "U.S. Economic Events" and find the links to Consumer Sentiment (for Michigan numbers) and Consumer Confidence (for Conference Board data) on the calendar, posted on the second Friday and last Tuesday respectively.

In addition, Briefing.com reports both indicators when they are published. The Federal Reserve Economic Database (FRED) at the St. Louis Fed provides basic details on the Michigan Consumer Sentiment data. The Conference Board information can be found at Conference-Board.org.

What to watch for: Increases (decreases) in consumer sentiment over several months.

What it means: Consumers feel exuberant (prefer taking it cautiously for a while).

What steps to take: Buy (short) retail stocks, starting (ending) with sellers of nondiscretionary items and ending (starting) with sellers of discretionary items.

Risk level: Low.

Profit possibility: $

4

EXISTING HOME SALES
Leading

(*See also* New Home Sales, Copper Price)

A N ENGLISHMAN'S HOME IS said to be his castle. For Americans, owning a home is *the* dream. Either way, home sales matter on so many levels. Because homes are such a massive part of many people's wealth, what happens in the housing market has an impact on the psychology and spending patterns of the nation.

That's why economists and money managers pay close attention to the National Association of Realtors' (NAR) reports on existing home sales. As the name suggests, the report indicates how many houses that had previously been occupied were sold during the month, and it typically represents the vast majority of activity in the housing market (the rest is sales of new homes). But it does much more than that!

"It contains the level of inventories and it gives the median price of a home in the country," says Joe Brusuelas, an economist at Bloomberg L.P. in New York.

The price of homes in general is important to the economy because of something known as the "wealth effect." What it means is that as house prices rise homeowners feel wealthier, and that affects how they view their future economic prospects. Specifically, when people feel wealthier, they spend more on average, even if their regular income has not changed in any way. But the sword cuts both ways. Falling home prices can have a negative impact by inducing people to cut their spending, sometimes drastically.

This whole phenomenon got out of control during the housing bubble of the mid–2000s. "Consumers increasingly relied on the increasing value of the homes to fund current and future consumption," says Brusuelas.

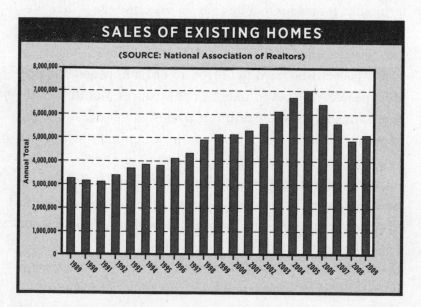

It wasn't that consumers just "felt" wealthier. They actually went to a bank and borrowed money against the increased value of their home to fund current consumption. In addition to the "wealth effect," there are other more direct impacts. "Typically when an individual buys a home, they buy new furniture, new housing wares, and new electronics," says Brusuelas. "In that way the sales of existing homes reverberate through the economy."

Investment Strategy

Historically, home sales have been key to the economic recovery. "In the ten postwar recessions, housing has been one of the leading drivers of a recovery," says Brusuelas. He says it should be intuitively obvious that this happens because the Federal Reserve, America's central bank, typically cuts interest rates during a recession.

For people who need to borrow to buy a house—and that's most people—the cut in interest rates reduces monthly mortgage payments and often results in a boost in sales. (Sales of automobiles typically get a boost from lower interest rates as well.)

In the wake of the housing bust of 2008 and onward, the big question is what role, if any, housing will continue to play in economic recoveries, says Brusuelas. It will play little role, he thinks, but maybe more than a mere cameo.

One trick to try to determine whether the housing market is likely to improve soon is to look at the level of inventories of unsold homes. In particular, look to see how many months it would take for all the homes available to sell at the current rate of selling. This is known as months of available inventory.

Clearly if the number of "months of inventory" is low, then that can augur an improving housing market and perhaps an improving economy. If it's high, then the reverse is true: perhaps a deteriorating housing market and a worsening economy.

EXEC SUMMARY: EXISTING HOME SALES

When to look: Existing home sales data is published at 10 a.m. ET around the 25th day of each month.

Where to look: *The Wall Street Journal* closely follows the housing market and publishes breaking news reports on sales of preowned homes immediately after the National Association of Realtors releases the data.

Go to *The Wall Street Journal* online's "Market Data Center" for a quick read of the data and how it compares to what investors were expecting. You'll find the data center at www.WSJMarkets.com. When you are there, you'll need to go to the "Calendars & Economy" section, look for "U.S. Economic Events," and find the links to "Existing Home Sales."

You could also go directly to the National Association of Realtors, which makes the data available at www.realtor.org/research/research/ehsdata. Other data worth looking at is pending home sales, or sales that are set to go through but haven't yet. It can be found at www.realtor.org/research/research/phsdata. Pending home sales data can provide clues about what activity is coming down the road in relatively short order.

What to watch for: Increases (decreases) in existing home sales and decreases (increases) in inventory levels measured in months of available property.

What it means: The economy is likely looking up (heading for the depths of hades).

What steps to take: If the housing market is perking up (and other metrics indicate a robust economy), buy economically sensitive investments, such as stocks.

If the opposite is happening—existing home sales data and other data point to a slowdown—avoid stocks in general (especially home builders and industrials) and hold cash or buy government securities such as U.S. Treasury bonds. If you must own stocks, go with those less sensitive to economic cycles, including companies that make consumer staples like shampoo and soap.

Risk level: Medium.

Profit possibility: $$

5

UNDEREMPLOYMENT OR SLACK

Leading Recession, Lagging Recovery

FORMER PRESIDENT BILL CLINTON sort of got it wrong when he adopted the campaign slogan, "It's the economy, stupid!" It should have read, "It's the jobs, stupid!" Why? Because for politicians a weak economy is synonymous with a lack of jobs.

It's important for investors too, but the widely reported raw unemployment rate is just too blunt a measure. We can learn much more—and make much more money—by digging deeper.

What's much more interesting is the underemployment rate, which measures how many people work part time because they can't find a full-time gig. This indicator is useful because it helps us to see into the future. For example, the number of employees working fewer hours than make up a normal workweek rises before actual layoffs begin. That's because managers are typically reticent about firing workers at the first sign of a business slowdown.

"You're going to try to preserve your workforce because you've trained them and there is a cost to training them," says Marc Pado, a market strategist at brokerage firm Cantor Fitzgerald in San Francisco. Managers know it can be hard to rehire and expensive to retrain new workers if the business lull turns out to be just a blip.

It is typically only when business has slumped off for an extended period that managers start to fire their workers. That lag makes tracking part-time work a very useful indicator of future unemployment.

Fortunately, the U.S. Bureau of Labor Statistics breaks out those workers who are working part time and specifies those who are doing so either because they could only find part-time work or because their employers cut back on the hours of work available. Collectively this is known as "slack." Economists are understandably more concerned about people who want to work more hours but can't than those who volunteer to work less.

Of course there are exceptions to the rule that part-time work rises before firing begins. Sometimes managers lay off workers without stepping them down to part time first. So an uptick in slack does not map on to future unemployment claims one-to-one. It is, however, a good indicator going into an economic slowdown. You can see the relationship in the chart below.

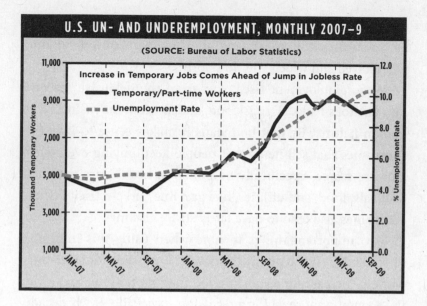

U.S. UN- AND UNDEREMPLOYMENT, MONTHLY 2007–9

(SOURCE: Bureau of Labor Statistics)

Increase in Temporary Jobs Comes Ahead of Jump in Jobless Rate

Temporary/Part-time Workers

Unemployment Rate

Coming out of a recession this indicator is less reliable. Some employers will hire workers part time before hiring them back permanently, but many will wait until they clearly need another set of hands full time before hiring again. So during recoveries it is best to check the employment report for growth in overtime. If overtime work is strong for several months, employers will likely start hiring new workers because they will be cheaper than paying time and a half to increasingly worn-out workers.

Investment Strategy

If you know changes in the level of unemployment are coming (because you have been assiduously watching the *underem-*

ployment numbers), then you can adjust how you invest. The key to success is in understanding which parts of the economy will do well and which will do poorly.

"As unemployment rises, you go to the defensive sectors," says Cantor's Pado. "Drugs, food, and alcohol: the mainstays of human nature." By that he means it makes sense to invest in companies that sell items that people keep buying even when jobs are scarce. Specifically he points to health care, pharmaceuticals, food, and utilities, like gasoline and electricity. These companies also tend to have fairly stable earnings.

Two important things to note when using this indicator: First, don't be faked out by the data. It is possible for temporary work to increase for a short period that has nothing to do with the economy approaching a recession, says Pado. Every decade, for example, the Census Bureau hires scads of temps but soon after releases them back into the employment pool. Make sure you are confident that the change in temporary working is reflective of the business cycle by looking at some of the other indicators in this book.

Second, Pado notes that when buying defensive stocks, it's about protecting your assets as the value of most stocks tend to fall going into a recession. "It's a matter of what goes down less," he says. Or put another way, defensive stocks will likely lose less than other riskier stocks.

EXEC SUMMARY: UNDEREMPLOYMENT RATE OR SLACK

When to look: The first Friday of the month at 8:30 a.m. ET.

Where to look: *The Wall Street Journal* closely monitors the jobs situation in the United States. All across WSJ.com, headlines and articles will detail the overall employment situation as soon as the data comes out.

To really get into the weeds for data on slack/part-time/underemployment, you'll be best served going directly to the Bureau of Labor Statistics's website, www.bls.gov, and searching for a table titled "Employed Persons by Class of Worker and Part-Time Status."

Note carefully: In early 2010, the BLS changed some of its statistics. Investors need to watch for such changes because statistics are only comparable from period to period if they are collected and presented in the same way each time. That matters because an unaware investor might mistake a change in the numbers for a real change in economic conditions when in reality it's just a change in collection method or presentation.

What to watch for: Increases in underemployment.

What it means: The economy is weakening.

What steps to take: Buy defensive stocks like drug makers (legal ones!), food, and alcohol.

Profit possibility: Low.

Risk level: $

INVESTMENT

(I)

THIS SECTION IS COMPOSED of eleven indicators that primarily track changes in business investment, which in this context means inventory on shelves and in warehouses as well as so-called fixed investments in buildings, vehicles, machinery, and even computer software. The construction of new residential housing, both single and multifamily, is also included in investment.

Business investment constitutes between 15 and 20% of GDP. That may seem trivial compared to consumption, but investment fluctuates massively, so it is very important "at the margin," which is where the action is. Consumers might cut back, but ultimately they have to consume food, clothes, and so forth no matter how bad the future looks. Businesses, by contrast, do not have to invest in *any* new plant, inventory, or software. Likewise individuals don't have to buy new houses. When the going gets rough, businesses cut way back or don't invest at all.

6

BOOK-TO-BILL RATIO
Leading

HALF A CENTURY AGO the idea of a computer in almost every home would have been the stuff of science fiction, with the emphasis on fiction. Now it's not only nonfiction—we have little computers in everything from watches and desktop and laptop computers to automobiles and telephones—but it's also big business.

Those little computers are powered by microprocessors, also known as chips or semiconductors, with a market estimated at between $300 billion and $350 billion globally in 2010, according to Trip Chowdhry, a technology analyst at San Francisco-based specialty research boutique, Global Equities Research.

Because semiconductors are used in so many cool gadgets, both at home and in the workplace, we can gain some insight into the health of the broad economy generally, and more specifically into some parts of the tech sector, by looking at the health of the semiconductor business.

It's relatively simple to measure the health of the chip business using the so-called book-to-bill ratio, which measures the relationship between bookings and billings.

Probably the best way to understand those two somewhat obscure business terms is to examine an example. If a company had orders for 100 microprocessors in a month, then the bookings, or booked sales, would be 100. But if during the same month only 80 chips were made and delivered, then the billings would be 80. The company bills the customer for the product only after it's shipped.

In this example, the book-to-bill ratio is 100/80, or 1.25. The company has an order backlog. That's frustrating for the customers but is actually a good position to be in for the chip manufacturer.

The Semiconductor Industry Association compiles a book-to-bill ratio for the entire industry, rather than just one company. That tells us whether the industry has an order backlog or is producing more chips than customers have ordered.

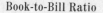

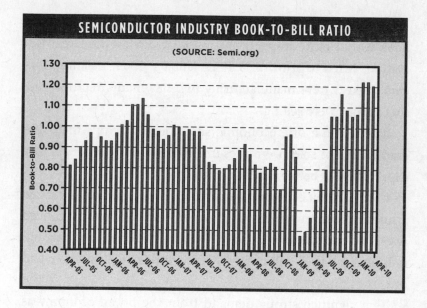

SEMICONDUCTOR INDUSTRY BOOK-TO-BILL RATIO

(SOURCE: Semi.org)

Investment Strategy

In the simplest terms, a book-to-bill ratio of 1.0 or higher is a favorable reading. It means that orders are greater than what the industry is able to fulfill.

"That says we are in an expansion," says Chowdhry. Or put another way, industry-wide there is a backlog of orders due to increased demand from the tech sector to make all those cool gadgets like PCs, iPads, cell phones, cars, and servers.

When times are bad, by contrast, chip makers have excess capacity, so they manufacture more chips than customers currently want. It's a bad sign for the industry and the overall state of the economy.

A quick look at the accompanying chart shows how the book-to-bill ratio dropped precipitously during the Great Recession. It fell to a low of 0.47 in January 2009, meaning that chip makers were manufacturing twice as many microprocessors as they were selling.

It reflected a dire economic situation. The chips that were made, but not sold, were presumably held in inventory in the expectation of better times to come.

It was a bleak economic picture, but the coming months saw a sustained improvement in the book-to-bill ratio that moved ahead of the whole economy. By July 2009 the book-to-bill ratio was above 1, indicating that the industry as a whole had order backlogs.

That signified strong demand from the broad economy as the world retooled and got back to work.

It's important to be careful when using this metric not to infer too much, specifically when looking at individual stocks. Chowdhry says a book-to-bill ratio over 1.0 is good, orders-wise, in the cell phone industry, the personal computer market, and the market for the computer servers that power the Internet. That's a useful data point to help build a thesis for buying an individual stock. But alone it's not enough, he says.

Another thing to remember with the book-to-bill ratio is that over time the inventory management philosophy has changed. Lean inventories are all the rage now in a way they weren't in the past, he says.

That means that over time, readings of the book-to-bill ratio might not be directly comparable, says Chowdhry.

Still, greater than 1 is a good sign.

EXEC SUMMARY: SEMICONDUCTOR BOOK-TO-BILL RATIO

When to look: Around the middle of the month for the prior month (mid-August for July data, for example).

Where to look: The Semiconductor Industry Association (SIA) publishes the book-to-bill ratio. Check out its website at www .sia-online.org. The same information can be found at www.semi .org.

What to watch for: Increases (decreases) in the book-to-bill ratio above (below) 1.00.

What it means: The economy is heating up (cooling down); the chip manufacturing sector is doing well (dying by degrees).

What steps to take: Buy (sell) chip manufacturer equities if, and only if, other indicators support the book-to-bill numbers.

Risk level: Medium or high.

Profit possibility: $$ or $$$ depending on the strategy chosen.

7

COPPER PRICE
Leading

I T'S AN INVESTING MAXIM that copper is the metal with a
PhD in economics. Why so? Well, it isn't really the metal
itself, but rather its price that is the smart part of the equation.

Broadly speaking, if the price is relatively high and rising,
then the industrial economy is doing well. If it's low and falling, then the manufacturing sector is hurting. Why? "Because,"
according to Frank Holmes, chief investment officer of San
Antonio–based U.S. Global Investors, "copper has unique
physical properties that make it the backbone of the industrial
economy." Holmes points out that copper prices are highly
correlated with the health of housing, infrastructure spending,
and manufacturing.

It works like this: The supply of copper is relatively stable
(and typically not too sensitive to changing price levels), so as

demand increases—for use in electrical wiring in houses or businesses—the price tends to go up. That's what makes the price so closely aligned with economic activity.

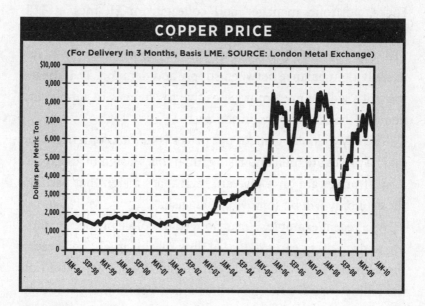

The good news is that this close relationship is likely to stay around for a while. Copper is one of the most cost-effective electricity conductors available and seems unlikely to be dethroned from that position anytime soon. (Gold is better at conducting than copper, but it's not cost-effective at all for most purposes. Aluminum, on the other hand, has a nasty habit of catching fire when used for wiring homes and offices.) As well as being used for wiring buildings, copper is also vital to the manufacture of automobiles and small electric appliances, where its electrical and heat conductivity is key.

Investment Strategy

Watching copper prices can help predict recessions, says Brian Hicks, portfolio manager and colleague of Holmes at U.S. Global Investors. In fact, Hicks goes a tad further, explaining that there is now (in the early twenty-first century) an extremely tight balance between supply and demand. That means the price will be even more sensitive to changes in supply and demand than it has been in the past.

The key to looking at copper prices is to look for a trend, he says. If prices are high and rising, then that's a sign of an expansion. If prices are on a plateau, then that's a sign that perhaps the economy will be somewhat sluggish.

As a recent example, Hicks noticed the price of copper starting to drop off in early 2010. He thought this might be because the Chinese economy was beginning to slow down. Based on the falling copper price as well as other factors that confirmed his suspicion, Hicks managed to dump his holdings of copper-related investments while the market was still cresting. By the time the market caught up to Hicks's view of the world and stock prices had dropped, he'd already sold out.

High prices are those around $3 a pound or $6,600 a metric ton. Under $2 a pound or around $4,400 a ton is considered low and is also below the price at which most new supplies of the metal can be developed, Hicks says.

A note of caution when watching the price of copper: Sometimes price spikes have little to do with improving economic conditions. Instead such movements can be caused by earthquakes, or industrial action by workers that interrupt the supply of the metal. Typically, prices fall back when full production is restored, not indicating a recession but rather a return to some normalcy in the copper market.

EXEC SUMMARY: COPPER PRICE

When to look: Every business day.

Where to look: Reporters of *The Wall Street Journal* keep a close eye on the industrial metals markets and file stories when noteworthy price changes take place.

If it's just the prices that you want, go to *The Wall Street Journal* online's Market Data Center at www.WSJMarkets.com. When you are there, you'll need to go to the "Commodities and Futures" section and look under "Metals."

Copper prices can be found in a slew of other places as well. The London Metal Exchange (LME), which dominates global trading in copper, has data available on its website, www.LME.co.uk. Likewise the COMEX division of CME Group also has data on copper prices. Also, prices can be found on www.KitcoMetals.com, a commercial website dedicated to providing metals market information.

The trick with whatever source of data used for copper prices is to make sure you use a constant benchmark price. On the LME it's the three-month price (i.e., the price now for metal delivered in three months' time); for COMEX, the benchmark delivery price moves around, making it tricky for the novice to get a handle on things.

For further reference, the World Bureau of Metal Statistics has a proprietary database at www.world-bureau.com/searchlink.htm. Also, investors on a budget can glean some historical data from the IMF's Primary Commodity Prices site at www.imf.org/external/np/res/commod/index.asp.

What to watch for: Increases (decreases) in copper prices, especially above $3 (below $2) per pound.

What it means: Housing and manufacturing are gearing up (headed for some tough times) and the economy along with it.

What steps to take: If you are sure the price movement is due to an increase (decrease) in demand and not a supply shock, invest in (get out of) copper and manufacturing stocks and rebalance your portfolio in favor of economic expansion (contraction).

Risk level: High.

Profit possibility: $$$

8

DURABLE GOODS ORDERS
Leading

W HEN IT COMES TO looking into the future we can learn a lot by looking at how businesses and consumers are spending on big-ticket items, or so-called durable goods.

For consumers, "durable goods" typically mean fridges, freezers, washing machines, and dishwashers. They are durable, which means they are expected to last awhile. They also typically cost a lot and so require that consumers have the confidence that shelling out a few hundred dollars on a single-use item won't leave them too short elsewhere in their budget.

For businesses, durables typically mean capital equipment. In layman's speak that means machines that can be used to make stuff that can be sold for a profit. It can also be aircraft, which are very big-ticket items, like Boeing 747s.

As with the consumer durables, orders for capital equipment are considered a measure of sentiment. If business equipment orders are high or rising, then that tells you the business community as a whole is getting more confident.

"It tells you people in business are putting their own money at risk," says Milton Ezrati, chief economist and market strategist at New York–based asset management firm Lord Abbett. "It's a good indication of where business is going."

More specifically, businesses likely wouldn't order new and typically expensive equipment if they didn't see a reasonable chance that they'd have enough customers to buy all the things the new machine was going to make.

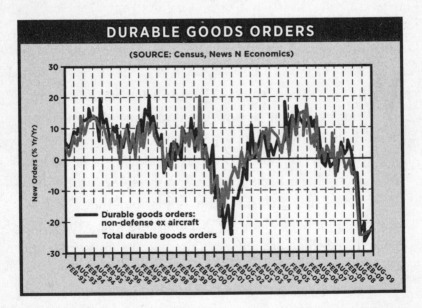

DURABLE GOODS ORDERS
(SOURCE: Census, News N Economics)

Investment Strategy

One important wrinkle is that the total durable goods orders indicator also includes very expensive defense products like warships and jet fighters. These items come and go at the whimsy of the government, so they typically don't tell us a lot about the economy, or rather the sustainable private sector economy.

Fortunately, it's easy to strip out those big Defense Department purchases. It's also easy to remove the impact of aircraft orders. They typically are so big and sometimes seemingly so random that they can play havoc when trying to interpret the data.

Ezrati notes that "even if you sweep away aircraft orders it is extremely volatile from month to month. It is very lumpy." That's why he suggests using a three-month and a five-month moving average as well as looking at the data from the prior month. That way you can see if the trend is being broken, he says.

In general, though, strong durable goods orders tend to be a bullish sign for stocks. "It helps support the general economy," says Ezrati.

Drilling down further, Ezrati says he pays particular attention to the capital equipment spending figures, which measure what businesses are doing rather than what they are saying. That's a rare look into the psyche of businesses that some other indicators don't give, he says. If Ezrati is convinced that a recovery is in the works, he tries to find suitable investments in stocks.

"If it's broad-based strength across the different components of durable goods, then that speaks to the general economy," he says. In such an instance it might make sense to look at investments tracking broad stock indices like the S&P 500 or perhaps look at those indices that focus on creating durable goods, like big manufacturing conglomerates such as General Electric (GE).

Even then, Ezrati says, it's important to keep an eye on the price of stocks. Or put another way, even if the economy is improving that doesn't mean overpriced investments are sensible.

EXEC SUMMARY: DURABLE GOODS ORDERS

When to look: At 8:30 a.m. ET around the 26th day of the month. The data covers the prior month.

Where to look: Editors and reporters at *The Wall Street Journal* watch the state of the durable goods market closely. As the data is released by the Census Bureau, *Journal* reporters file breaking news stories for WSJ.com.

If it's just the data you want, go to *The Wall Street Journal* online's "Market Data Center" at www.WSJMarkets.com. When you are there, you'll need to go to the "Calendars & Economy" section and look under "U.S. Economic Events" for "Durable Goods Orders."

Alternatively you can go straight to the source: The U.S. Census Bureau, at www.census.gov/manufacturing/m3/. Historical data is here: www.census.gov/manufacturing/m3/historical_data/index.html.

For a simplified and easy-to-use version, try Briefing.com's Economic Calendar in its free "Investor" section.

What to watch for: Increases (decreases) in durable goods orders, excluding defense and aircraft purchases, over three to five months.

What it means: The economy is likely to grow (shrink) in the near term.

What steps to take: Go long (short) a broad basket of stocks like the S&P 500. Alternatively, the more adventurous investor might consider buying (selling) specific durable goods manufacturers like General Electric (GE).

Risk level: Medium to high, depending on the investment strategy chosen.

Profit possibility: $$ or $$$ for the stock pickers.

9

HOUSING PERMITS AND STARTS
Leading

(*See also* Copper Price, New Home Sales)

Buying a house is a big purchase for most people. For some others it's just plain massive. That's why they call owning your own home the American dream. Note the "dream" part of that: For many it will remain just as unreal as a dream.

Houses are a special case of consumer durables because they are expected to last years and years. From start to finish, they typically take at least a year to build.

The reason we look at this pair of indicators is that an increase in the number of housing permits applied for and the commencement of building those houses (known as "starts") signals confidence in the economy over the near and the medium term. After all, builders usually don't construct new houses unless they are fairly sure that people will have the confidence to buy them. Remember, most people borrow the money to buy a house and doing so shows that purchasers are optimistic that they will keep their jobs and income for a sustained period of time.

During the depths of a recession the cost of borrowing money is typically quite low and that can mean that buying a house is cheaper than renting one. That's how the cycle starts: Cheap money lures in home buyers, and home builders know this so they construct houses in anticipation.

Increases in the number of housing starts and housing permits that have been issued clearly indicate that increases in overall economic investment are in the offing as builders buy lumber, bricks, cement, roofing materials, pipes, and so forth. In short, the housing business can turn the lights back on in many different industries.

It works vice versa too. During most economic expansions the cost of borrowing money increases as the economy gets healthier. That has the knock-on effect of slowing new building and so slowing the economy down.

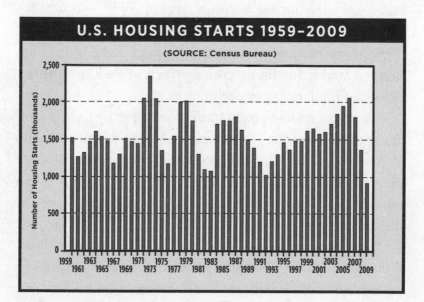

Investment Strategy

Typically, the number of building permits issued and the level of housing starts begin to increase *before* the economy improves. A sustained pullback in the sector typically comes *ahead* of an economic slowdown or a recession. That movement ahead of the changes in the overall economy is the reason we think of housing construction as a *leading* indicator.

(Note: Although housing usually begins to improve ahead of the economic cycle, that didn't happen during the economic expansion that got under way in 2009. That was because of the exceptional nature of the housing bubble that preceded the Great Recession. Here we present what normally happens because we want this book to be useful across many business cycles, not just the most recent.)

There are many ways to profit from the ups and downs in the housing market. But the first thing to do is to work out whether the sector is improving or declining.

"Don't just look at one month's worth of data; instead look at the trend," says Vinny Catalano, chief investment strategist at New York–based Blue Marble Research. Catalano suggests that investors look at a few months' worth of data at a minimum to be sure that the trend is real before looking where in the stock market to invest.

The obvious first place that will do well in a housing recovery is the home-building companies themselves. Catalano points to the SPDR S&P Homebuilders (XHB) exchange-traded fund as a good first port of call. The value of the so-called XHB is determined by the value of a basket of the shares of companies that build houses. As the housing sector does well, so do these stocks. The so-called basket approach makes sense for most people because it takes away the risks of picking the wrong stock even if you got the sector correct.

Catalano cautions, however, that the value of stocks is determined by other factors as well, such as interest rates and the overall economic climate. "Prices of home-building stocks can zoom up in anticipation before the data confirm the recovery," he adds. In addition to home-building stocks, Catalano also says it makes sense to look at other sectors. For instance, he suggests considering lumber companies that make house framing materials and miners that dig up copper to make electrical wiring.

EXEC SUMMARY: HOUSING PERMITS AND STARTS

When to look: At 8:30 a.m. ET around the 16th of the month. The data covers the prior month.

Where to look: *The Wall Street Journal*'s editors and writers watch the housing market closely. As news about housing permits and starts comes out, *Journal* reporters file breaking news stories for publication on WSJ.com.

If it's just the data that you want, go to *The Wall Street Journal* online's "Market Data Center" at www.WSJMarkets.com. When you are there, you'll need to go to the "Calendars & Economy" section and look under "U.S. Economic Events" for "Housing Starts."

For the permits data you'll need to go the source, the Census Bureau, the same folks responsible for keeping track of how many Americans there are. The data can be found at www.census.gov/const/www/newresconstindex.html.

What to watch for: Increases (decreases) in building permits over several months.

What it means: The economy is heating up (cooling down).

What steps to take: Buy (short) home-building stocks directly or an ETF like the SPDR Homebuilders (XHB).

Risk level: Medium for the ETF, high for picking individual stocks.

Profit possibility: $$ or $$$

10

INDUSTRIAL PRODUCTION AND CAPACITY UTILIZATION

Coincident, Leading

THE WAY SOME RABBLE-ROUSERS and politicians bemoan the state of the industrial economy you'd be forgiven for thinking that manufacturing of goods of all types was on its last legs in the United States. Well, it's not dead yet. The value of industrial output totals about $1.7 trillion, or more than one-tenth of GDP. It's still a significant and vital part of the overall economy.

That's why both savvy investors and pointy-headed economists alike pay close attention to the health of the manufacturing sector. They do so by looking at two closely related economic indicators: industrial production and capacity utilization. We present them together here.

Industrial production (IP) measures how much physical stuff is produced in the economy each month. IP includes everything from prescription medicines, telephone handsets, and

TVs to ingots of gold, bars of steel, and planks of wood. It is considered a coincident indicator since typically it neither leads nor lags the state of the overall economy.

By contrast, capacity utilization compares actual industrial production with the absolute maximum amount of stuff industrial companies could produce if they ran every single factory flat-out all the time. (Phew! It sounds exhausting.) Capacity utilization is reported as a percentage figure with a maximum possible utilization of 100%. This indicator also does a good job of measuring the current state of the industrial economy: The higher the percentage utilization, the healthier the economy is right now. Increases in the percentage utilization rate are seen as a good sign for businesses because it means companies are not letting machines and other assets sit idle.

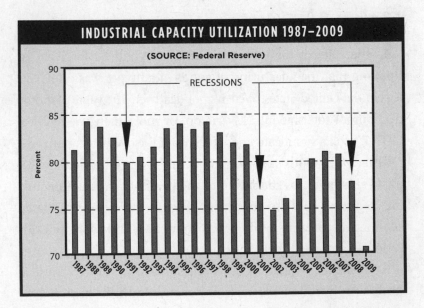

Investment Strategy

It's easy to see how capacity utilization and industrial production rise and fall with the state of the overall economy. Utilization rates fell meaningfully during the recessions of 1990–91, 2001, and 2008–9. It's notable that utilization only started increasing a month after the recession ended. The following table shows monthly data. The recession is indicated by the shaded areas:

YEAR	JAN.	FEB.	MARCH	APR.	MAY	JUNE	JULY	AUG.	SEPT.	OCT.	NOV.	DEC.
2000	82.3	82.4	82.4	82.6	82.5	82.3	81.8	81.4	81.5	80.9	80.7	80.1
2001	79.3	78.6	78.1	77.7	76.9	76.2	75.7	75.2	74.7	74.1	73.6	73.5
2002	73.7	73.6	74.1	74.2	74.5	75.2	74.9	75.0	75.0	74.9	75.2	74.9

Capacity utilization can also be used to help see the future in two ways: First, high levels of CU tend to signal future business investment, possible employee hiring, and new orders for capital equipment (new machines to make even more stuff). As businesses move closer to maximum capacity, business chiefs find themselves less and less able to manage with their current resources.

"Companies bridge the gap by hiring people and getting bigger or better machines," says Bill Stone, chief investment strategist at PNC Wealth Management in Philadelphia.

The companies that supply industrial machinery do well in this environment. "Think about who supplies capital equipment," says Stone, pointing to Cummins Inc. (CMI), ABB Ltd. (ABB), Fluor Corporation (FLR), and their competitors as prime examples. It's worth noting that this industry tends to see big cyclical swings in earnings and stock prices. So timing is the key for investors, he says.

In addition to considering individual companies, investors might also want to look at exchange-traded funds that track a basket of stocks in the sector such as the Vanguard Industrials ETF (VIS). This isn't an exact match for the sector, but it is broadly close.

The second way this information can be used to forecast: "When capacity utilization gets near its upper ranges you need to start worrying about cost pressures, [or rising prices for input materials]," explains Stone. Although theoretically utilization can reach 100%, the reality is the figures typically don't exceed the mid–80s. When utilization neared 90% in the 1970s, cost pressures soared, notes Stone.

Why? The closer companies come to running their factories at full capacity, believes Stone, the more comfortable they feel in increasing the prices they charge to customers. But when all companies do that there may be an overall bump in costs.

"It might cause you to favor commodity-based companies that would benefit from rising raw materials costs rather than those that would suffer from increased costs," says PNC's Stone. Two investments that could do well under such circumstances: the Vanguard Materials ETF (VAW) and the iShares S&P North American Natural Resources ETF (IGE), both of which track a basket of underlying stocks tied to natural resources and commodities.

EXEC SUMMARY: INDUSTRIAL PRODUCTION AND CAPACITY UTILIZATION

When to look: At 9:15 a.m. ET around the 15th of the month. The data is for the prior month.

Where to look: Editors and writers at *The Wall Street Journal* watch industrial production closely. As news about it and capacity utilization is released, *Journal* reporters file breaking news stories for publication on WSJ.com.

If it's just the data that you want, go to *The Wall Street Journal* online's "Market Data Center" at www.WSJMarkets.com. When you are there, you'll need to go to the "Calendars & Economy" section and look under "U.S. Economic Events" for "Industrial Production."

Alternatively, you can find data on industrial production and capacity utilization at the Federal Reserve. Find the most recent data at www.federalreserve.gov/releases/g17/current. Historical data is available at www.federalreserve.gov/releases/g17/current/table11.htm.

What to watch for: Increases (declines) in capacity utilization.

What it means: Business investment is rising (falling) and the economy will soon follow.

What steps to take: Buy (short) capital equipment suppliers like Fluor (FLR) or appropriate ETFs.

Risk level: Medium to high.

Profit possibility: $$ to $$$

11

INSTITUTE FOR SUPPLY MANAGEMENT (ISM) MANUFACTURING SURVEY

Leading

(*See also* Philadelphia Fed: Business Outlook Survey, Industrial Production and Capacity Utilization)

MANUFACTURING IS NOT AS large a percentage of the economy as it once was, but it is still important enough that much of the investing world pays close attention to one particular survey out each month: the ISM Manufacturing Survey. It measures the health of the manufacturing sector of the economy from the perspective of the purchasing managers who work at manufacturing companies throughout the United States.

Purchasing managers are vital to any manufacturer because without them there would be no raw materials in place to fabricate into finished and semifinished products. These managers spend much of their time trying to predict the raw materials needs of their organizations. They then make decisions about how much of what stuff to purchase from other companies.

For instance, the purchasing managers at Ford Motor (F) may need to buy steel, paint, glass windshields, and tires (among many other things) in order to make cars. They buy enough of those materials to build the number of cars the company thinks it will be able to sell in the coming months. As a result, how purchasing managers feel about the state of their business reveals a lot about the overall state of the economy.

The Institute for Supply Management (ISM) surveys four hundred companies in twenty major industries about new orders, production, employment, supplier performance, inventories, prices of materials, back orders, imports, and exports. From the data on new orders, production, employment, supplier performance, and inventories it creates a Purchasing Managers Index (PMI), the ISM survey's headline figure.

Investors should look to see whether the PMI is in expansion or contraction territory, explains Sophia Drossos, a strategist at New York–based investment bank Morgan Stanley. A figure above 50 indicates an expansion in the sector. A figure below 50 indicates a contraction.

One important note: The Institute for Supply Management was previously named the National Association of Purchasing Managers (NAPM). So, if you see references to NAPM in old newspaper reports you'll know what it means.

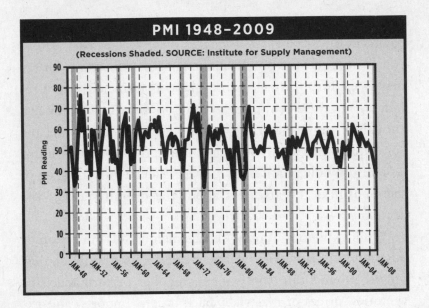

Investment Strategy

When analyzing the ISM index it's important to dig deeper than just the headline figure. That's because while the headline figure is important, the subindices can be even better indicators of what is going to happen.

"You can look at the new orders [index] as a leading indicator for future economic activity," says Drossos. In other words, if new orders are strong, or above 50, then future activity is likely to be good also.

She also points to the "employment index" as a fair gauge of the health of the market for manufacturing jobs. Again, a figure over 50 shows growth in manufacturing employment.

"When those [the headline figures, new orders, and employment] are expanding at the same time, that's consistent for growth in the manufacturing economy," she says. Drossos also adds that such an environment would favor so-called high-beta assets, meaning those investments that are sensitive to changes in the health of the economy. Specifically, a healthy and expanding manufacturing sector usually means stocks would do well and bonds would do poorly.

EXEC SUMMARY: INSTITUTE FOR SUPPLY MANAGEMENT (ISM) MANUFACTURING SURVEY

When to look: The report is available on the site at about 10:00 a.m. ET on the first business day of the month.

Where to look: Editors and writers at *The Wall Street Journal* watch the ISM data closely. As news about it and capacity utilization are released, *Journal* reporters file breaking news stories for publication on WSJ.com.

If it's just the data that you want, go to *The Wall Street Journal* online's "Market Data Center." You'll find it at www.WSJMarkets .com. When you are there, you'll need to go to the "Calendars & Economy" section and look under "U.S. Economic Events" for "ISM Manufacturing."

Alternatively, you could go to the source, the Institute for Supply Management's website, www.ism.ws. It has the manufacturing survey information available to anyone with access to the Web. In addition, www.Briefing.com provides a summary of the data in a timely manner at about the same time. Although much of the site is for subscribers only, the "Investor" section is free and for most purposes it's adequate.

What to watch for: Increases in PMI, orders, and employment above the break-even level of 50.

What it means: The manufacturing sector is growing and likely the economy along with it.

What steps to take: Go with high-beta securities like many stocks, especially those heavily tied to manufacturing.

Risk level: High.

Profit possibility: $$$

12

INSTITUTE FOR SUPPLY MANAGEMENT (ISM) NON-MANUFACTURING SURVEY
Leading

(*See also* ISM Manufacturing Survey)

T HERE ARE A LOT of businesses that don't actually make anything in America. It's strange but true. Think about it. Retailers sell food to you but don't grow it. Brokers help you to buy real estate but don't construct it. Filling stations sell you gasoline but don't refine it from crude oil.

Banking, retailing, wholesaling, and the nonconstruction parts of the real estate business, like Realtors, are all services and they are a big deal to economists and investors because they make up about seven-tenths of the private (nongovernment) economy in terms of both employment and GDP, explains Kurt Karl, chief U.S. economist at insurance giant Swiss Re in New York.

That's why the Institute for Supply Management's monthly nonmanufacturing survey, frequently called the ISM Services

Index, is so important. "It represents what's going on in the services sector from the purchasing managers' viewpoint," says Karl.

The ISM Services Index is easy to read too, just like its sister index, the ISM Manufacturing Survey. The headline figure for the nonmanufacturing survey is a single number known as the Business Activity Index.

"Above 50 is meant to be growth in the services sector," says Karl. Likewise, below 50 indicates a contraction or slowing in the nonmanufacturing part of the economy.

"The 50 figure is not perfect, however: We don't have a long enough history to know if that is correct," adds Karl. The ISM Services data only goes back to the late 1990s, in contrast with the manufacturing data, which goes back to the 1930s. That lack of history is seen as a potential weakness for the services data. However, it does come out very soon after the end of the month and so lots of economists like Karl tend to overlook that drawback.

One bigger problem Karl points out is that purchasing managers are nowhere near as important in services as they are in the manufacturing sector. For instance, the amount of paper a bank needs to order gives you little clue as to how healthy the company is, whereas the amount of coal and iron ore a steelmaker orders very much tells you how well that firm is doing.

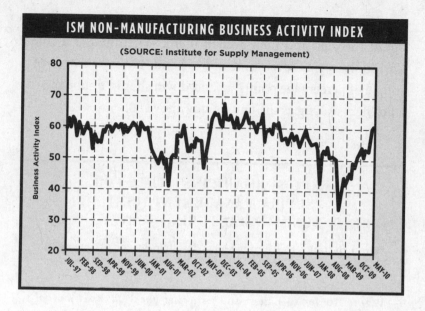

Investment Strategy

Karl says he likes to look at the "new orders" figure as it is "more forward looking" than the headline figure. Or in other words, the new orders figure tells you more about the future state of the service sector than does the headline ISM Services figure.

By the same token, export orders are an important indicator of future economic activity. If one or both of new orders and export orders show consistent readings over 50, then you can be "reassured" that the services sector will likely see growth in the near future if it isn't growing already.

As ISM Services Data is relatively new, Karl warns that it has a tendency to jump around like one of those beans from

Mexico. That's at least part of the reason he likes to make charts out of the data and then eyeball them. When he has a chart, Karl looks for a "level" and not a trend. He says moves of a couple of percentage points up and down should not be seen as a problem as long as the figures stay above 50.

EXEC SUMMARY: INSTITUTE FOR SUPPLY MANAGEMENT (ISM) NON-MANUFACTURING SURVEY

When to look: The third business day after the end of each month at about 10:00 a.m. ET.

Where to look: Editors and writers at *The Wall Street Journal* watch ISM Services Data closely. As news about it is released, *Journal* reporters file breaking news stories for publication on WSJ.com.

If it's just the data that you want, go to *The Wall Street Journal* online's "Market Data Center" at www.WSJMarkets.com. When you are there, you'll need to go to the "Calendars & Economy" section and look under "U.S. Economic Events" for "ISM Non-Manufacturing."

Alternatively, go straight to the Institute for Supply Management's own website at www.ism.ws, where the data and commentary are freely available. See also Briefing.com, as referenced previously for other indicators.

What to watch for: Increases (decreases) in new orders and/or the headline figure above (below) the putative break-even level of 50.

What it means: The service sector is probably growing (shrinking) and the economy along with it.

What steps to take: Now is the time to purchase (sell) riskier assets like stocks and to sell (purchase) old, recession-proof standbys like government bonds.

Risk level: Low.

Profit possibility: $

13

JoC-ECRI INDUSTRIAL PRICE INDEX
Leading

(See also Copper Price)

S OMETIMES TO GET A read on the economy you need to get down and dirty. In this case that means taking a look at a hodgepodge of gritty industrial commodities. Ugh? Well maybe not, because a lot of the dirty work has already been done by the compilers of the helpful JoC-ECRI (*Journal of Commerce*-Economic Cycle Research Institute) Industrial Price Index.

It might be obscure, but the way the JoC-ECRI signals changes in the industrial economy certainly isn't. That part of the economy isn't as big as the service sector, but it's a lot more cyclical. That's good news for economic forecasters because it means changes in that sector can be much easier for forecasters, economists, and investors to identify.

The JoC-ECRI Industrial Price Index measures the prices of

key industrial commodities that go into making all the stuff produced in the economy. As industrial companies increase their purchases of these materials, the prices get bid up, signaling an expansion. As they decrease their purchases, the prices pull back, foreshadowing a slowdown or even perhaps a recession. The net result is that the prices of industrial commodities act as a leading indicator to the economy as a whole.

The index includes energy prices, base metals (like copper, tin, steel, nickel, and aluminum), textiles, and a miscellaneous category (including tallow, rubber, and plywood).

Random as that list might seem, the elements on it were not randomly picked. In the early 1980s, the guys at the New York City–based Economic Cycle Research Institute, which spends all its time studying how different parts of the economy change through the business cycle, went to great lengths to include only commodities with prices that are sensitive to changes in the economy.

For that reason, ECRI excluded agricultural commodities, where prices tend to shift based on weather, and precious metals, where price movements are sometimes based on speculation and not industrial use, explains Lakshman Achuthan, managing director at ECRI.

On top of that, ECRI made another critical decision. Not all of the commodities picked would be traded on futures exchanges, although about half of them, like copper, are.

The reason? "Normally it doesn't matter, but once in a while commodities become a hot investment class and that leads everyone and their brother to pile in," Achuthan explains. "They can get really volatile."

If the index included only exchange-traded commodities, then a jump in the indicator could falsely indicate a coming economic boom when the reality was a speculative fervor, he explains. Having about half the components not traded on exchanges helps guard against false reads in the index, he says.

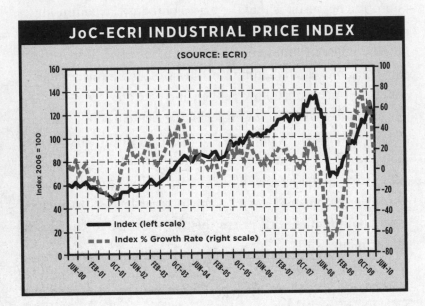

Investment Strategy

ECRI's Achuthan says he likes using this index because it's really sensitive to changes in the economy and because it moves substantially. The trick, he says, is to chart the index and then he says a turn in the economy will be "undeniable."

For instance, when the economy rebounded from the Great Recession, the JoC-ECRI Industrial Price Index ran up 50–

60%. That sort of move helps give you "the conviction to go against the consensus," he says.

But making a call on a turn in the economy from expansion to recession or slump back to boom needs more than a chart. Achuthan says it's important to follow the ECRI analytical philosophy of making sure that the move in the index is pronounced (i.e., it moved a lot), persistent (it continues to move in that direction), and pervasive (it's not just driven by one component of the index). If the change in the index moves according to these "three P's," then it's probably safe to call a turning point in the economy.

The good news for investors is that the stocks that produce such industrial materials tend to move as violently as the underlying commodities. Or put another way, swings in the price of commodity-chemicals maker DuPont (DD) will be larger than those of companies like Proctor & Gamble (PG), a manufacturer of consumer staples like toothpaste.

EXEC SUMMARY: JoC-ECRI INDUSTRIAL PRICE INDEX

When to look: Weekly.

Where to look: ECRI provides its up-to-date JoC-ECRI IPI to its members for a fee. Alternatively, *Barron's* magazine publishes the IPI data each week. Again, you'd have to pay for a subscription, but if you need up-to-date data in a timely manner, then that may be the way to go.

However, if you have more time than money it probably pays to scour the press for nuggets. ECRI's Achuthan says that one way or another about 70% of the information on ECRI's outlook available through media sources. The company tries to keep an archive of press coverage on its website at www.BusinessCycle.com/news/press.

What to watch for: The three P's (pronounced and persistent movement in the index driven by a large—or pervasive—number of industrial commodities).

What it means: The overall economy is about to soar (tank).

What steps to take: Buy (short) industrial stocks.

Risk level: High.

Profit possibility: $$$

14

LONDON METAL EXCHANGE INVENTORIES

Leading

(*See also* Copper Price, ISM Manufacturing Survey)

SOME SMART INVESTORS LOOK at the price of copper as a clue to the health of the economy. That's great stuff to know, insofar as it goes. But how cool would it be if you could predict the price of copper and other metals?

The way some savvy investors do this is to look at the amount of material that isn't being consumed and just remains idle. Or put another way, how many tons of copper or of aluminum are just sitting in global stockpiles? It's counterintuitive, but it's important.

Traditionally, there has been an inverse relationship between inventory levels and prices. When inventories are low, then prices have typically been high or rising. It works vice versa also.

The problem has always been that it's hard to get a true read on what inventories throughout the economy really are. For instance, how many tons of copper does the wire maker in Brooklyn, New York, really have in his shed? Individually, such things tend not to make much difference, but when all the little players are added up, their collective importance emerges.

In other words, getting good data to analyze metals markets is tricky. One clue to solving the puzzle is found at the London Metal Exchange, a commodity futures organization that dominates the global trading in futures-style contracts of industrial metals such as copper, aluminum, zinc, lead, tin, and nickel. Each business day the LME provides data on the amount of metal that is available in its warehouses.

To be sure, it isn't the whole picture of worldwide metals inventories. But it is transparent (i.e., what you see is what you get), timely (daily), and, in our opinion, a good index to monitor.

Note carefully: Very low interest rates can distort the traditional inverse relationship between prices and inventories. When the cost of borrowing money is abnormally low—like during the Great Recession of 2008–9 and its aftermath—speculators sometimes decide to snap up commodities as an investment. As a result, inventories stay high when prices do also. That's in part because the metal owned by speculators isn't available for fabrication by manufacturers.

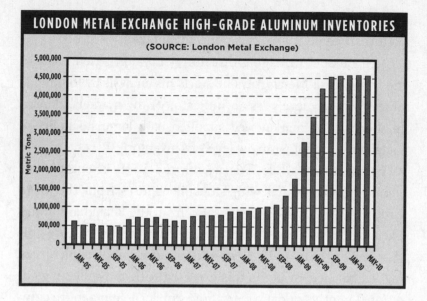

Investment Strategy

The size of LME inventories can indicate a lot about the future health of the metals and mining business. If inventories are high, then it's likely a sign that business will slow down as miners and refiners cut back on production. Likewise, if inventories are low, then it could portend a future pickup in business for miners and refiners.

There is a wrinkle: Data about most commodities, including metals, can be a bit murky. But that means the savvy investor who is prepared to put in some legwork can really win big. Why? Because the data situation is equally cloudy for all involved and most won't go to any extra effort to get a clearer picture. If you do, you'll have the advantage.

Neil Buxton, managing director at London-based consulting firm GFMS Metals, says he starts his analysis by looking at LME inventory levels "as an indicator of the market balance." In short: Is the market well supplied with large stockpiles of metal, or is it tight with low levels of inventories?

In any event, while it is useful, the LME inventory data should be augmented with stockpile figures from the CME Group's COMEX division and also from the Shanghai Futures Exchange, says Buxton. Their statistics are similar to those provided by the LME and help provide a more complete picture of market balance. By doing this extra legwork and collecting additional nuggets of data, smart investors can gain a more complete picture of the murky world of metals.

On top of that, savvy investors should look at indicators that reflect possible future demand. In particular, Buxton says he watches the various Purchasing Managers indices, or PMIs, like the ISM Manufacturing Survey described elsewhere in this book. These PMIs tell us what manufacturing businesses are planning to do in the near future. If business conditions look good to the purchasing managers, then that will likely be good for metals demand.

In addition, the health of the Chinese economy has been a very important factor in determining metals prices. Buxton says that China represents 30–40% of global demand for some of these metals, and he notes that trade data from that country frequently impact metals prices.

"When looking at these markets, the underlying fundamentals do matter, and that comes through," he says.

EXEC SUMMARY: LONDON METAL EXCHANGE INVENTORIES

When to look: Every business day.

Where to look: The London Metal Exchange provides price, inventory, and other market data on its website, some free, some for a fee at www.lme.co.uk. The COMEX and the New York Mercantile Exchange are now a division of the CME Group at www.cmegroup.com. The Shanghai Futures Exchange website shows weekly data on inventory levels at www.shfe.com.cn.

What to watch for: Increases or decreases in inventories of different types of metal. In addition, look for increases or decreases in Chinese demand and the relative health of the manufacturing sector in the industrialized economies (see various Purchasing Managers indices).

What it means: Typically, low inventories signal a thriving manufacturing sector. High inventories signal a stagnating manufacturing sector (except when interest rates are abnormally low).

What steps to take: When inventories are high, typically avoid stocks that are sensitive to the manufacturing economy. When inventories are low, buy manufacturing stocks.

Risk level: High.

Profit possibility: $$$

15

PERSONAL SAVINGS RATE
Coincident

FOR MANY AMERICANS IT'S kind of boring to save. Why bother when you can spend now and pay later? Anyway, it keeps the economy revving along, right?

Well, almost. "Savings today can help longer-term growth in the future," explains Derek Burleton, deputy chief economist at TD Bank Financial Group in Toronto.

In short, more savings in an economy means more investment. That money has to go somewhere, and, in this case, it gets from your savings account into loans and securities that finance the construction of new factories or the retooling of old ones.

Savings are important to economists for this reason, but they are also often difficult to calculate because the so-called personal savings rate isn't actually tracked anywhere. Instead, statisticians back into the number by looking at the overall income of all people in the United States and then subtracting overall spending. They assume that if you earned it but didn't spend it, then you must have saved it.

It's also worth noting that a high savings rate in a country can help protect a government that is deep in debt. For heavily indebted governments, the big question is: Where is the money going to come from? Well, if the money comes from savers within the country, then there is much less to worry about.

At the time of writing, Japan's government is heavily indebted, with borrowings of about 200% of its national output or GDP. That's about twice the level of U.S. government indebtedness, percentage-wise anyway. But here's the thing: In some ways the Japanese government has less to worry about than the U.S. government does. While Japan—a nation of big savers—mostly borrows from its own people, the United States is heavily dependent on foreigners lending it the money. Americans are not as thrifty. As a result, the Japanese government doesn't have to worry that foreigners will suddenly stop lending to it, while the U.S. government is constantly on guard.

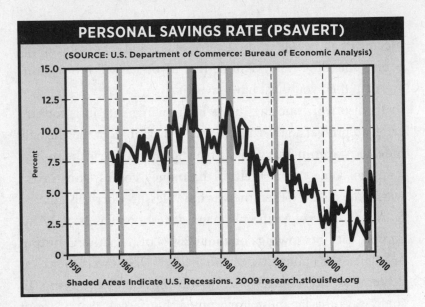

PERSONAL SAVINGS RATE (PSAVERT)

(SOURCE: U.S. Department of Commerce: Bureau of Economic Analysis)

Shaded Areas Indicate U.S. Recessions. 2009 research.stlouisfed.org

Investment Strategy

There is a big problem with the savings rate data. It's very volatile. That's because of the way it's calculated. Burleton explains that the income and spending figures are both just estimates. On top of that, they are both very large numbers. Because significant errors can be made in the estimates, the derived savings rate numbers can often jump around violently.

"We try not to read too much into levels of savings—more the direction," says Burleton. Or, in other words, he looks at whether the savings rate is going up or down, rather than whether it is 3% or 1.5%.

He says investors can use the trend in the savings rate to

assess the mood of consumers. If the trend is for more savings, then consumers are probably pretty nervous. If the trend shows progressively lower levels of savings, then it's a good sign that consumers have the confidence to spend.

EXEC SUMMARY: PERSONAL SAVINGS RATE

When to look: At 8:30 a.m. ET about four weeks after the month reported. It comes in the form of the "Personal Income and Outlays" report from the Commerce Department.

Where to look: Editors and writers at *The Wall Street Journal* look closely at the data on income and spending, the raw materials of the savings figures. As the data is released, reporters file breaking news stories for publication on WSJ.com.

If it's just the data you want, go to *The Wall Street Journal* online's "Market Data Center." There you'll find summary data on personal income and outlays. You'll find the data center at www .WSJMarkets.com. When you are there, you'll need to go to the "Calendars & Economy" section and look under "U.S. Economic Events" for "Personal Income and Outlays."

For a derived "savings rate" figure as well as the income and spending numbers, go to the U.S. Bureau of Economic Analysis at www.bea.gov/national/index.htm#personal. For historical data, try the St. Louis Fed's FRED database.

What to watch for: An increase (decrease) in the savings rate.

What it means: Consumers are probably pretty jittery (feeling confident).

What steps to take: If the savings rate is trending upward, then it's likely that the consumption part of the economy will be weak. Therefore, it's best to avoid stocks of consumer-driven companies.

Risk level: Medium.

Profit possibility: $$

16

UNIT LABOR COSTS

Coincident

(See also ISM Manufacturing Survey,
Philadelphia Fed: Business Outlook Survery)

SOME WORKERS ARE LAZY or unproductive and some are hardworking and efficient. Anyone who has held a job knows that. Although sometimes on an individual-by-individual basis that phenomenon can be hard to measure, overall we can know how efficient we are by looking at something called "unit labor costs."

This indicator measures the cost of the labor component of making a unit of industrial output. Probably the best way to think of it is: How much of the cost of making a single widget was from labor?

Over time what businesses really want to see is declines in unit labor costs. Such an event means that businesses are being more efficient. And that, in short, is what unit labor costs are: a measure of efficiency and productivity.

"Better machines mean better productivity, and that will manifest itself in lower unit labor costs," says Campbell Harvey, professor of finance at Fuqua School of Business at Duke University. "But the changes in productivity don't happen quarter to quarter; they are more of a long-term function." If there is a noticeable change in unit labor costs over a period of, say, three years, some of that might be attributable to improvements in productivity, says Harvey.

The exact opposite of what most businesses want happened in the 1970s and early 1980s (see figure below), when unit labor costs soared, sometimes over 10% a year. It was the result of high wage inflation.

If this indicator sounds complicated, don't worry too much. The Bureau of Labor Statistics, a government agency, calculates it for you by dividing employer labor costs (wages and benefits) by real value-added output. If workers produce more value and their wages stay the same, unit labor costs will fall, which is good for businesses.

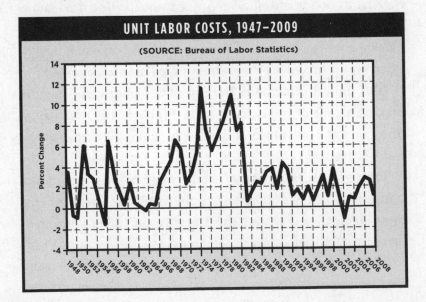

UNIT LABOR COSTS, 1947–2009

(SOURCE: Bureau of Labor Statistics)

Investment Strategy

The biggest wrinkle with the unit cost data is not in reading whether labor is getting more or less efficient. By now that should be easy. Rather, the real knotty problem is determining what it means for the broader economy. The big issue: Exactly the same phenomenon means precisely opposite things depending on where you are in the business cycle, explains Harvey. Talk about diabolical! For that reason, you need to look at this metric in conjunction with other indicators, like those in this book, to tell where you are in the business cycle.

If you are in a recession and unit labor costs are driven up, it could be a good thing. The reasoning: It may be a sign that workers are being paid better. That can eventually show up in increased demand for goods and services. So under those circumstances investors might view rising unit labor costs as a positive sign of an economic rebound. Sagging labor costs during a recession, however, could also signal deflation and an even deeper downturn to come.

Conversely, in an economic boom, rising labor costs might be considered bad. The reason: It might be a sign of inflation. Specifically, if the labor cost component of making stuff goes up and the materials cost stays the same, then businesses must increase selling prices in order to maintain the same level of profit. Lower labor costs that are the result of improving worker efficiency during an economic boom, however, would be a very bullish sign. As Harvey recommends, it makes sense to consult the other indicators in this book.

If it looks like the economy is improving and the unit labor costs are falling, then investors might want to consider purchasing assets that are sensitive to the economy, like stocks, especially manufacturing companies.

For investors who don't want to pick individual stocks, an investment fund that tracks a basket of industrial stocks, like the Industrial Select Sector SPDR (XLI) exchange-traded fund, might make sense.

EXEC SUMMARY: UNIT LABOR COSTS

When to look: This data is published quarterly at 8:30 a.m. ET near the beginning of the month. The data is for the prior quarter and comes out in February, May, August, and November. Each also has a revision one month after the first read.

Where to look: Reporters and editors of *The Wall Street Journal* closely watch labor trends. As news is released by the Labor Department, Journal reporters file breaking news stories for publication on WSJ.com.

If it's just the data that you want, go to *The Wall Street Journal* online's "Market Data Center." You'll find the data center at www .WSJMarkets.com. When you are there, you'll need to go to the "Calendars & Economy" section and look under "U.S. Economic Events" for "Productivity and Costs."

To see the data directly, go to the U.S. Bureau of Labor Statistics at www.bls.gov/bls/newsrels.htm and look for "Productivity and Costs" news release.

What to watch for: Changes in unit labor productivity.

What it means: This all depends on where the business cycle is.

Rising labor costs during a recession might signal a recovery or a nasty bout of inflation. Falling labor costs might mean higher productivity or a deep recession.

What steps to take: If a recession you see, safety you must seek. A real expansion of the economy should be anticipated by a move into riskier assets, like equities. But if the expansion is merely nominal due to inflation then take some Treasury Inflation-Protected Securities (TIPS) and mine for gold (or buy a gold ETF).

Risk level: Low to high depending on how well you integrate this indicator with others to discern the economy's true direction.

Profit possibility: $ to $$$$

GOVERNMENT

(G)

GOVERNMENT HAS A VORACIOUS appetite for consumption of all kinds of stuff. Together, all the durable and nondurable goods, services (like research and development and education), and investment in equipment (much of it military), buildings, and highways account for about 15–20% of GDP.

We've included only one indicator of its activity: the federal government budget deficit. It's a particularly interesting indicator because while in the short run deficits often point to increases in the government component of the economy—and hence increases GDP—they also portend problems ahead for other parts of the economy.

Notably, when the government has big deficits it typically results in decreases in the consumption (C) and investment (I) a little further in the future. That is because as government expands it does so usually by a combination of increasing taxes, borrowing, or printing paper money. Taxes of course decrease future consumption and investment. Borrowing is nothing more than future taxation, and printing money causes inflation, which also acts as a form of tax, albeit a silent one.

Taxes are necessary evils, the price we pay for civilization, in the words of Supreme Court justice Oliver Wendell Holmes (and the IRS), but they can be very distorting. As well as inducing strange architectural designs (to avoid taxes on windows), huge households (to diminish the impact of a tax on households), and big format newspapers (to decrease a tax on the number of pages), poorly designed taxes have wrecked economies. It usually takes some time to do so and isn't a business cycle phenomenon, but we figured that while we are at it we should warn investors that big deficits (and the inevitable changes in the tax code) are worth worrying about.

17

FEDERAL GOVERNMENT BUDGET DEFICITS AND THE NATIONAL DEBT
Coincident to Leading

SOME PEOPLE HAVE MONEY left at the end of the month, but these days most people find that they have more month left at the end of their money. Well, if you feel a bit strapped for cash these days, don't despair, as you are not alone. National governments are too.

When government spends more money than it receives in the form of tax revenues, the result is called a deficit. It's like a gaping hole in the budget. To fund the deficit, governments borrow, and the accumulated borrowings form the national debt. At the time of writing, the U.S. national debt totaled over $14 trillion. That's a fourteen with twelve numbers after it. It's a whole lot of money, and it could become a problem.

The reason deficits, and ultimately national debt, are worrisome is because the bigger the debt gets, and the higher interest rates on government bonds go, the heavier the burden of the government's debt service. In other words, a greater portion of each tax dollar must go just to pay interest on the debt.

Also problematic, governments that became too heavily indebted have often resorted to printing money. While that helps them pay the debts, it ultimately causes inflation.

To make matters worse, while it's easy to see consequences of running large deficits, it's actually quite difficult to interpret deficit data. The trouble with looking at one year's deficit of any country in isolation is that a government's tax revenue is highly correlated to the business cycle. In a recession the government tends to bring in fewer tax revenues, and in a boom year it takes in much more. That's why you can't give any one year's deficit any real meaning, says David Ranson, head of research at Beverly Farms, Massachusetts–based economics consulting firm H. C. Wainwright & Co. Economics Inc. He says it's better to look at the annual deficit as a percentage of GDP. The key number is 3%.

"It's convention to regard 3% as a normal deficit because the economy grows 3% normally," says Wainwright's Ranson. "That means the government's debt is rising only as fast as GDP, which is healthy."

In other words, it isn't a big deal if the national debt stays at a constant percentage of GDP. But what if deficits grow faster than the economy?

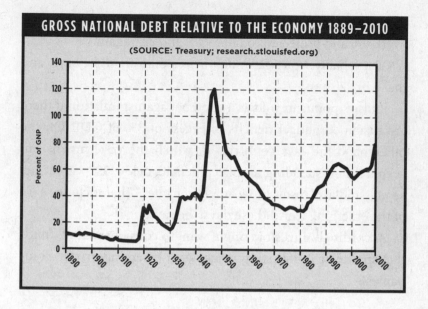

GROSS NATIONAL DEBT RELATIVE TO THE ECONOMY 1889–2010

(SOURCE: Treasury; research.stlouisfed.org)

Investment Strategy

The national debt is a harbinger of inflation, but its level is not correlated with the business cycle. Annual budget deficits, however, are closely tied to the business cycle. "Over time, the higher your deficit, then the higher are inflation rates, and you could get hyperinflation rates if the government is unable to extricate itself from that predicament," explains Ranson. Or put another way, continual deficits lead to a rising national debt, and a high level of national debt is a harbinger of inflation. As already mentioned, the key to avoiding inflation is for average annual deficits to stay below 3%. The problem is that, based on projections at the time of writing, the current U.S. deficit is over 10% and projected to fall to 4% and rise again.

"It probably won't get much better than that," he says, and that worries him.

Ranson points to gold as a good bet against inflation if there are sustained budget deficits in excess of 3% of GDP. On the other hand, he says countries in which the government can keep a lid on spending and keep deficits below 3% will attract capital and as a result grow at a faster rate. "That includes a lot of the emerging world these days," he says.

Accordingly, investors might want to consider mutual funds that specialize in investing in stocks of emerging market companies.

EXEC SUMMARY: FEDERAL GOVERNMENT BUDGET DEFICITS AND THE NATIONAL DEBT

When to look: For deficit figures, the U.S. Treasury provides monthly statements of its receipts and outlays at 2 p.m. ET on the 8th business day of each month.

In addition, continuous estimates for the national debt are available via various national debt clocks like US Debt Clock.org at www.usdebtclock.org/.

Where to look: Editors and writers at *The Wall Street Journal* keep a close eye on the finances of the U.S. government. As the U.S. Treasury releases its data, reporters file stories for publication on WSJ.com.

For a look at the data, you can go straight to the U.S. Treasury monthly statement at www.fms.treas.gov/mts/index.html. To analyze it appropriately you'll need to annualize the monthly data (i.e., sum up the prior twelve months of deficits) and then compare that total to overall GDP.

In addition, the FRED database at the St. Louis Federal Reserve enriches us with historical data at http://research.stlouisfed.org/fred2/series/FYFSD?cid=5, and major news outlets also cover budget negotiations. If you want to take an in-depth look at the current federal budget, browse www.whitehouse.gov/omb/budget/.

What to watch for: Increases (decreases) in the national debt as a percentage of GDP, usually signaled by recurring deficits greater than 3% of national income.

What it means: The government's incentive to cause inflation is increasing (decreasing).

What steps to take: Short (buy) traditional government bonds and buy (short) gold, and/or emerging market equity mutual funds.

Risk level: High.

Profit possibility: $$$

NET EXPORTS

(NX)

THE UNITED STATES DOESN'T exist in isolation. We sell stuff to foreign countries and buy stuff from them. In short, the rest of the world does count. That's why we include half a dozen indicators of net exports here.

The difference between what we sell abroad (exports) and what we buy (imports) is called net exports. Economists use the symbol NX.

For small, open economies like Ireland, NX is positive and a major contributor to GDP. For America, however, NX is typically negative, shrinking GDP by about 5–10%. Improvements generally entail NX becoming less negative, but still below zero. Exports and imports, it should be noted, not only include merchandise but also services such as tourism, consulting, and banking.

The biggest influence on U.S. net exports is the dollar. When the greenback is weak, exports improve, and the net position becomes less negative because U.S. goods look cheap to foreigners. Likewise foreign goods look expensive to Americans. Therefore, exports increase while imports decrease. It works vice versa too.

In the short term, economic theorists tell us, the biggest influence on exchange rates is interest rates, or rather the expectation of changes in relative interest rates. Longer-term exchange rates respond to relative changes in the real economy, things like prices and productivity. To understand what is going to happen to exchange rates, one must know what is happening on the ground in the world's other major economies, which also happen to be America's biggest trading partners. That is why we have also included international and foreign indicators in this section.

Such indicators can be used to get a feel for developments in the global economy. In times past, one country or region could suffer recession while another boomed. Today, we're all connected—a phenomenon eloquently discussed by author Thomas Friedman and others.

18

BALTIC DRY INDEX
Leading

THE FUNNY THING ABOUT the Baltic Dry Index (BDI) is that it involves lots of water. Specifically, it's a measure of the price of moving raw materials across the world's oceans. In that sense the BDI is quite wet. The "dry" refers to the state of the things shipped: iron ore, coal, and grains, typically. They are dry cargoes, as opposed to wet ones like crude oil.

The "Baltic" part of the moniker refers to the London-based Baltic Exchange, which calculates and publishes the BDI weekdays. It's not limited to cargoes shipped across the Baltic Sea, however. The Baltic Exchange tracks the cost of moving freight along key shipping lanes around the globe. The index it creates reflects the cost to rent a ship today in the so-called spot market, rather than a price to rent one at some point in the future.

These so-called dry-bulk ships are really like "massive oceangoing dump trucks," says Urs Dur, senior equity analyst for marine shipping and logistics at Lazard Capital Markets in New York. How big? The largest of these vessels is so big it can't sail through either the Panama or the Suez Canal. In order to traverse the globe these oversize ships must travel around the Cape of Good Hope or Cape Horn at the bottom of Africa and South America, respectively. As a result these ships are called "Capes." Other ship categories in descending order of size are Panamax, Supramax, and Handysize, all of which can move through the canals and are included in the BDI along with the Capes.

The simplest way to think about movements in the BDI is that it goes up and down according to the demand for the vessels. As demand increases, the price to charter a ship rises. That's because in the short run, the number of ships available is typically fixed. So when the global economy hums and the need for raw materials increases, the price to rent a ship rises.

We track the BDI because it gives an insight into the state of trade in the most basic industrial materials. Notably, iron ore and coal together make steel—an essential input for construction and a key to the manufacture of automobiles as well as many other consumer durables.

Lately that means watching China. Lazard's Dur says he watches Chinese iron ore inventories and the overall health of that economy. In particular, when iron ore inventories are low but the Chinese economy is still healthy, increased imports of ore might be in the cards.

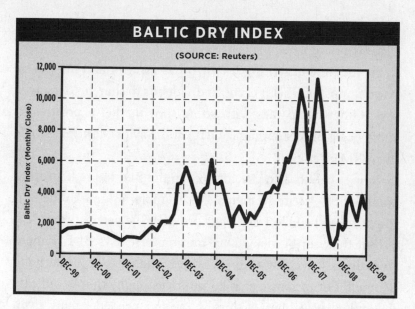

BALTIC DRY INDEX
(SOURCE: Reuters)

Investment Strategy

Dur says investors can profit from changes in the BDI by finding a publicly traded shipping company with revenues that fluctuate day to day just like the BDI. Such a company would see its revenues increase as the BDI rises, and its earnings fall as the BDI sinks.

Finding such a company is easier said than done because some shippers lock in the rate at which they rent out their vessels for years at a time. The result: Their revenue gyrates less than does the BDI.

One company that fits the bill is Baltic Trading Ltd. (BALT). Dur says the firm's stated goal is to rent out ships at spot market rates, rather than locking in prices with multiyear contracts. "This is a pure Baltic play," he says.

At the time of writing the firm has no debt and intends to pay out most of what it earns in dividends to shareholders, Dur says. Other companies with some spot market exposure include Eagle Bulk Shipping (EGLE) and Navios Maritime Holdings (NM), he says.

Some analysts also use changes in the BDI to predict future commodity-price movements. For example, a slump in the BDI might suggest a falloff in metals prices in the near future.

But that can be risky, Dur cautions. He says BDI changes sometimes have little to do with changes in underlying demand. For instance, a spike in prices might simply indicate the limited availability of ships in the area needed. At any given moment, the supply and demand for ships is local. If an available ship is halfway around the world from where it's needed that can cause a price spike in charter rates, but it will be only temporary.

Another wrinkle to watch for: a drop in the BDI caused by newly manufactured vessels hitting the water. They will likely weigh down on charter rates for all ships, regardless of underlying demand for the cargoes.

EXEC SUMMARY: BALTIC DRY INDEX

When to look: Each business day.

Where to look: The underlying data is produced by the Baltic Exchange in London at www.balticexchange.com/, but there is a fee if you want the data.

Alternatively, you can snag a chart from InvestmentTools.com at www.investmenttools.com/futures/bdi_baltic_dry_index.htm, or look at the public sites of the major wire services.

What to watch for: Increases (decreases) in the BDI.

What it means: Increased (decreased) demand for raw materials used in manufacturing.

What steps to take: Buy (short) publicly traded shipping companies that are exposed to daily fluctuations in the cost of renting dry-bulk ships.

Risk level: Medium.

Profit possibility: $$

19

BIG MAC INDEX
Leading

I N 1986 A JOURNALIST at *The Economist* newspaper in
London wondered what different currencies, like the Japanese yen or the British pound, would be worth if a Big Mac
burger cost the same in every country. The idea became the Big
Mac Index (BMI).

"The Big Mac Index was an amusing way to make economics more fun," says Pam Woodall, a senior economics writer at
the publication, and the inventor of this indicator. "People
loved it and we kept doing it year after year."

While it looks strange at first glance, there is some serious
economics behind it: the theory of purchasing power parity
(PPP). This theory says that if international trade is unfettered,
then goods and services in all countries should eventually cost
approximately the same amount. In this case the "good" of

choice is the ubiquitous Big Mac burger sold by fast-food retailer McDonalds. If Big Macs cost three euros in France and three dollars in New York, then the logical exchange rate, according to the PPP theory, should be one dollar = one euro.

The beauty of using the Big Mac is that they are (more or less) identical everywhere they are sold. That means no adjustments need to be made for differing quality or size, as would be the case with nonstandard goods.

To the extent that the actual price of the burger in another country differs from prices in the United States, that country's currency is either overvalued or undervalued.

If the same Big Mac costs fifty cents in Beijing but three dollars in New York, then by this indicator's reckoning the Chinese currency is undervalued.

BIG MAC INDEX

Local Currency Under (-)/ Over (+) Valuation against the Dollar

Big Mac Price*, $	Country	-50	-25	0	25	50	75	100
6.87	Norway							
6.16	Switzerland							
4.62†	Euro Area							
4.06	Canada							
3.98	Australia							
3.75	Hungary							
3.71	Turkey							
3.58‡	United States							
3.54	Japan							
3.48	Britain							
3.00	South Korea							
2.99	United Arab Emirates							
2.86	Poland							
2.67	Saudi Arabia							
2.56	Mexico							
2.44	South Africa							
2.39	Russia							
2.37	Egypt							
2.36	Taiwan							
2.28	Indonesia							
2.16	Thailand							
2.12	Malaysia							
1.83	China							

* At market exchange rate on March 16th
† Weighted average of member countries.
‡ Average of four cities

SOURCES: McDonalds; *Economist*.

Investment Strategy

The most useful investing idea behind the Big Mac Index is to predict the value of foreign currencies over the long term. Lately a big question in foreign exchange markets and policy circles has been whether the Chinese currency, the yuan, is undervalued. A quick look at the 2010 Big Mac Index provides a definitive answer. Not only is the yuan undervalued, it is the *most* undervalued currency—possibly by as much as 50%. By the same measure, the Mexican peso is also undervalued by over 25%.

So should you invest in currencies that are undervalued according to the BMI?

The Economist's Woodall says some people claim that the Big Mac Index is a better predictor of the value of a currency than more sophisticated economic models. She also notes that many academic studies show its validity.

But Woodall cautions that there is a wrinkle that distorts the BMI. The problem: Although Big Macs are sold like any other good, they can't really be stored for use weeks later. We know. One of us tried and it doesn't end happily. That makes the Big Mac more like a service, something to be consumed where it's purchased like a back massage. So what? Well, there are sound economic reasons why services should be cheaper in emerging markets: Wages are cheaper there and wages are a big cost component in services. So the price of a Big Mac should be somewhat cheaper in Beijing than in New York.

It also means that even when currencies are fully valued, the BMI will show that emerging-market currencies are undervalued. So use this indicator as a guide to whether currencies are egregiously overvalued or undervalued. If a currency is vastly undervalued, expect it to rise in value, eventually. Vice versa, if it's overvalued expect its value to fall.

If these caveats about *The Economist*'s Big Mac Index make

you nervous, UBS Wealth Management Research has developed a BMI variant: It calculates the number of hours a local worker must toil to purchase a Big Mac. A decrease in the number of hours might indicate an increase in productivity and hence an eventual appreciation of the domestic currency. Careful though—other things can have an impact on how fast a worker earns the value of a Big Mac, like changing tastes or downward market pressure on retail prices.

If you decide you do want to invest in currencies, a safe way to go is to look at the various exchange-traded funds that track the value of different currencies relative to the U.S. dollar. Examples include CurrencyShares Euro Trust (FXE), CurrencyShares British Pound Sterling Trust (FXB), and the CurrencyShares Canadian Dollar Trust (FXC). There are other families of ETFs that serve a similar role. Novice investors would do well to avoid investing directly in the currency markets or trading with borrowed money.

EXEC SUMMARY: BIG MAC INDEX

When to look: Weekly on Fridays, when *The Economist* is published.

Where to look: The online version of *The Economist* newspaper, Economist.com, publishes the Big Mac Index.

What to watch for: Countries where Big Macs cost significantly less (more) in dollar terms than they do in the United States.

What it means: The local currency is undervalued (overvalued) and hence likely to appreciate (depreciate) in the long run.

What steps to take: Buy (short) undervalued (overvalued) currencies, possibly through a currency ETF.

Risk level: Astronomical.

Profit possibility: $$$$+

20

CURRENT ACCOUNT DEFICIT
Leading

(See also TIC Data)

T O SAY THAT U.S. consumers love imported goods would woefully understate the situation. No, the truth is that for at least the past two decades Americans have gorged themselves on imports, notably from China. As a result, gigantic imbalances have emerged in the global economy.

The problem, however, is not in itself that Americans buy lots of foreign knickknacks. Buying stuff is what makes the world economy go round. The issue is that Americans have spent so much more money on foreign products than foreigners have spent on U.S. goods and services. Such a situation can persist for years but not forever.

We can measure exactly how much more stuff the United States buys from other countries than foreigners buy from us by looking at the so-called trade balance or the "current account."

For most countries the trade balance is roughly equivalent to the current account. In the national accounts the current account is technically the trade balance plus net income from interest and dividends plus net foreign aid. So when pundits and economists talk about a current account deficit they almost always really mean a trade deficit, something America has run for many years.

"We pay for those imports by borrowing money or by selling assets to the rest of the world," says Paul Wachtel, professor of economics at NYU Stern. In some ways this is like selling the family silver to put food on the table. You can do it once, but it's not sustainable.

Because the United States has run a relatively high trade deficit for so long, a huge imbalance has built up, explains Wachtel. Specifically, he means that foreigners have lent America a lot of money to finance the purchase of those imports. That can spell trouble ahead for the value of the U.S. dollar and the health of the overall economy.

"The more we do that, the more years we are accumulating debts to the rest of the world," says Wachtel. "Then the question comes up: 'Gee, can you pay the interest on those debts and can you pay them back?'"

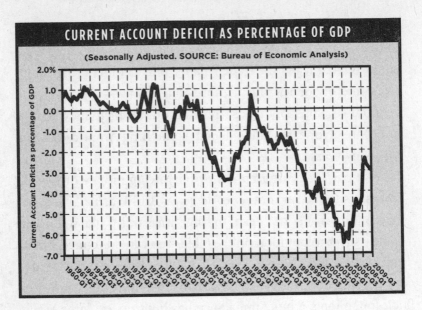

CURRENT ACCOUNT DEFICIT AS PERCENTAGE OF GDP

(Seasonally Adjusted. SOURCE: Bureau of Economic Analysis)

Investment Strategy

The real key to making sense of the current account deficit is to look at its size relative to that of the overall economy. In addition it must be looked at over a period of time and not just at one moment. That's because the trade balance tends to fluctuate with the business cycle.

Typically a trade balance improves coming out of a recession and worsens going into one. So it's more important to look at the trend than a single month of data.

Wachtel says a good rule of thumb is that a healthy ongoing trade deficit is under 5% of annual GDP for a country. When it's bigger than 5%, it can be a problem.

"When we look at smaller emerging market countries it's a strong indicator of a looming exchange rate crisis," says Wachtel. Or in simpler terms, the value of a country's currency could fall precipitously if the current account deficit exceeds 5% of GDP. He points to Hungary as a recent example of a country that had a current account deficit of about 10% of its GDP right before a rapid currency depreciation. He also notes Greece had a similar problem.

The other side of the equation, says Wachtel, is that countries with consistent trade surpluses tend to attract more capital from investors and, as a result, have faster-growing economies. That should mean that emerging market economies with big surpluses will grow fast in the future and that might be a good place to invest.

America has historically been a special case when it comes to the trade balance because of the special role of the U.S. dollar as the world's reserve currency. That has meant the United States has been able to have decades of surging imports (and hence massive trade deficits) without precipitating a currency crisis.

But lately people have begun to ask the question: Can this trade deficit go on forever? "It might not," says Wachtel. "If you go down the road five or ten years, things might change." Or, in other words, if the United States doesn't fix the trade balance problem relatively soon, the value of the dollar could drop—a lot.

EXEC SUMMARY: CURRENT ACCOUNT DEFICIT

When to look: The current account data is released once a quarter at 8:30 a.m. ET around the middle of the month, March, June, September, and December.

Where to look: Editors and writers at *The Wall Street Journal* closely monitor the current account data. When it's released by the Commerce Department, *Journal* reporters file breaking news stories for publication on WSJ.com.

If it's just the data that you want, go to *The Wall Street Journal* online's "Market Data Center" at www.WSJMarkets.com. When you are there, you'll need to go to the "Calendars & Economy" section and look under "U.S. Economic Events" for "Current Account."

Alternatively, try the FRED database at the St. Louis Federal Reserve, which has lots of historical data.

What to watch for: Trade deficits greater than 5% of GDP (except for the United States).

What it means: An exchange rate crisis may loom.

What steps to take: Short that country's currency.

Risk level: Astronomical.

Profit possibility: $$$$+

21

OIL INVENTORIES
Leading

MUCH AS FORMER U.S. vice president Al Gore or President Barack Obama might want it to happen, America has little chance of kicking its addiction to oil anytime soon.

The entire industrial complex is an oil-guzzling monster: Try getting to work, heating your home, running a factory, or buying anything without using any oil. Heck, half the stuff in our homes—for example, anything made out of plastic—is made from it!

Because our lives depend so heavily on our oil use, the oil market is considered a superb and sensitive barometer of the health of the U.S. economy. Fortunately for the budding economist and would-be trader there is a wealth of information on the energy market. Notably the Energy Information Administration, part of the U.S. government, provides regularly updated details of the energy business.

Specifically, each week (usually on Wednesdays) the EIA releases data on the level of energy inventories. Or put another way, it tells the world how much crude oil, gasoline, and fuel oil (plus other products refined from oil) are on hand and available for use. The beauty of this regular release of data is that analysts can compare the stockpile levels week to week.

"Low oil inventories and/or a big draw down in those inventories [from week to week] is generally economically positive," says Edward Meir, a senior commodities analyst at New York–based futures broker MF Global. "It means you have strong industrial production, with factories using energy, utilities using energy, people driving to work, flying, and boating."

He says that's just how things were in 2007 and 2008. During that time inventories were drawn down, and the price of crude oil reached a record of $147 a barrel, a level that remains a record at the time of writing in 2010. Meir also notes that such high prices eventually crimp demand as people seek to avoid the cost of higher energy costs.

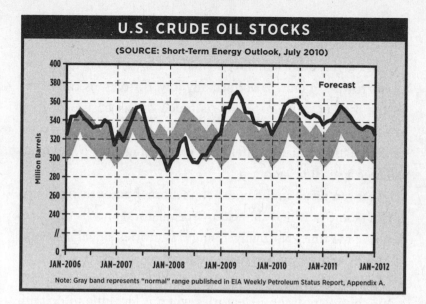

U.S. CRUDE OIL STOCKS

(SOURCE: Short-Term Energy Outlook, July 2010)

Note: Gray band represents "normal" range published in EIA Weekly Petroleum Status Report, Appendix A.

Investment Strategy

When watching the oil inventory figures that come out each Wednesday, Meir says the key item to watch is the crude oil inventories (sometimes referred to as stocks) that exclude the government's strategic petroleum reserve (SPR). The SPR is not easily available for use unless the government decides to release some and so it doesn't really represent a potential source of supply.

Meir also says market expectations play a big part in reaction to the EIA data. If, for instance, oil inventories are expected to fall by a certain amount and they fall by less, then that can be seen as a sign that the economy is weaker than previously thought. Likewise, a bigger draw down than forecast can lead people to believe that the economy is ahead of where investors seemed to think it was.

One commodities market wrinkle to watch: When the cost of borrowing money is abnormally low, distortions can occur in the market, explains Meir. As much of the cost of owning commodities is in having capital tied up, when borrowed capital is cheap speculators often find it advantageous to buy oil as a hedge against inflation.

That can result in the unusual phenomenon of rising inventories (some of which are held by speculators) and rising prices at the same time. Normally, rising inventories signal a surplus of supply and go hand in hand with falling prices.

Another wrinkle to watch for is temporary supply interruptions causing a dip in inventories when it has little to do with the underlying economic fundamentals. Such events can include refinery explosions, wars, drilling moratoriums, and shipwrecks. To be clear, while these things will affect the market price and inventory levels, such events frequently don't reflect the health of the underlying economy.

EXEC SUMMARY: OIL INVENTORIES

When to look: The weekly data is released Wednesday at 10:30 a.m. ET.

Where to look: Markets editors at *The Wall Street Journal* closely watch oil inventory data. When the EIA releases the data, *Journal* reporters file breaking news stories for publication on WSJ.com.

If it's just the data that you want, go to *The Wall Street Journal* online's "Market Data Center" at www.WSJMarkets.com. When you are there, you'll need to go to the "Calendars & Economy" section and look under "U.S. Economic Events" for "EIA Petroleum Status Report."

Alternatively, you can get the information yourself at www.EIA.gov.

What to watch for: Increases (decreases) in oil inventories (not counting the government's strategic reserves).

What it means: Demand is probably weakening (strengthening) due to underlying weakness (strength) in the overall economy.

What steps to take: Cyclically appropriate investments. That means avoid (embrace) risky investments like stocks. Sell (buy) stocks that are sensitive to economic conditions, like industrial companies.

Risk level: Medium.

Profit possibility: $$

22

TANKAN SURVEY
Leading

I F YOU ARE OVER thirty, you might just remember a time when Americans trembled in fear that the Japanese were going to buy up all of America's landmarks and that Japan Inc. would annihilate U.S. businesses. It didn't turn out that way.

It seems funny now after two decades of stagnation, but Japan is still important. It's estimated to be the third-largest economy in the world, just behind China, which, by virtue of its enormous population, edged its way into the number two slot in 2010. However, while China's economy may be larger now, Japan's is actually more important in some ways. That's because on a per person basis, Japan is vastly richer. It means that when Japanese consumers decide to spend money it can have a big impact on the global economy.

For anyone wanting to get a deep understanding of the Japanese economy, the Tankan Survey is the best place to go. Every quarter, Japan's central bank asks businessmen in about nine thousand small, medium, and large firms what they think about business conditions in Japan and what their expectations are regarding future changes in prices, sales, employment, and exchange rates as well as credit conditions. It's probably the most comprehensive economic indicator on the planet. In some ways it's like a giant Japanese version of the Institute for Supply Management's surveys on manufacturing and services.

The main Tankan Survey index, the business conditions diffusion index, is easy to read: Anything above zero is seen as positive or indicative of economic growth, says Kurt Karl, an economist in New York for insurance giant Swiss Re. Likewise, a reading below zero, negative, is indicative of a slowdown or recession, he says.

Karl describes the survey as "wide and deep," meaning there is lots of information for economists to dig into should they feel the desire.

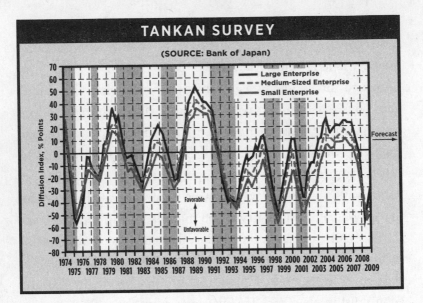

TANKAN SURVEY

(SOURCE: Bank of Japan)

Investment Strategy

If you are interested in investing in Japan, the Tankan is a fantastic leading indicator. The accompanying graph shows Japanese recessions in light gray, and the lines show the business community's read on the economy, broken down by small, medium, and large businesses. Together these business executives called recession and recovery in advance, sometimes only by a little but sometimes, as in 1990–94, well ahead of time, and with no false signals.

Not only is the Tankan a great leading indicator but it also takes on greater weight than it would in other countries because in Japan some other government data isn't as reliable as, say, in the United States. For example, Karl notes that Japan's

GDP figures are subject to what would elsewhere be considered wild revisions. "It's something you struggle with when forecasting Japan's economy," says Karl.

He points to an instance of strong positive growth for Japanese GDP eventually being revised to a contraction, or negative growth. Or in other words: A strong expansion was later revised into being a recession. That's pretty ridiculous if you ask us.

Not only does the Tankan Survey not get revised, but it also is a very reliable indicator of the health of Japan's economy, Karl says. In fact, he prefers it to the government's GDP figures.

You can learn a lot from just reading the headline numbers of the Tankan Survey. But you can learn even more by digging deeper and really getting into the weeds. There are separate data series for the different parts of the economy. For instance, in addition to the headline Tankan data there is also information that relates solely to the manufacturing sector.

Karl says his favorite piece of the Tankan Survey is the manufacturing indicator. He says it's "the best indicator of the health of the whole economy."

He also says that while the overall quality of the Tankan data is good (and better than the government's GDP data), the quality of the data that is submitted by the country's large manufacturers is even better. That's in part because it's easier for manufacturers to measure output than it is for managers working in the service sector.

When there is a clear indication of improving economic growth ahead it can make sense to look to invest in Japanese stocks. Small investors, or those without the resources to research individual Japanese stocks, might consider the iShares

MSCI Japan Index (EWJ) exchange-traded fund. It tracks a basket of Japanese stocks. There are other similar products available from other companies as well.

EXEC SUMMARY: TANKAN SURVEY

When to look: The beginning of April, July, and October, and mid-December, at 8:50 a.m. Japanese time (that's either 6:50 p.m. ET or 7:50 p.m. ET, depending on the season).

Where to look: The data is posted in *The Wall Street Journal* data center as it is released. You'll find the data center at www.WSJ Markets.com. When you are there, you'll need to go to the "Calendars & Economy" section and look under "International Economic Events" for "Tankan Survey."

Alternatively, you can go to the Bank of Japan, which creates and publishes the Tankan Survey. Thankfully it puts out an English version at www.boj.or.jp/en/type/stat/boj_stat/tk/index.htm. Another important indicator for Japan is the Industrial Production report, which can be found here at www.meti.go.jp/english/statistics.

What to watch for: Survey results in positive (negative) territory.

What it means: The Japanese economy is going to grow (shrink) soon, regardless of what official government stats might say.

What steps to take: Buy (sell) some Japanese stocks or ETFs.

Risk level: High (due to exchange rate uncertainties mostly and Japan's overall poor economic performance since ca. 1990).

Profit possibility: $$$

23

TIC DATA
Leading

(*See also* Current Account Deficit, Federal Deficit)

A MERICANS LOVE TO SPEND, not just consumers but the government also. It's been a big part of what has made America the way it is. But the big dirty secret is that none of this would be possible to quite the extent it has been if it weren't for a willingness by foreigners to lend us the money to do it.

If foreigners weren't eager to lend, then you can be sure we'd all have to pay a lot more to borrow money for everything from credit card balances to mortgages and car loans. Or the value of the U.S. dollar would have to be a lot lower to boost our exports and curb our seemingly insatiable desire for oil and Chinese-made stuff.

That willingness by foreigners to lend us money is quantified in dollar terms in the Treasury International Capital, or TIC, data.

TIC gives us a snapshot of the flows of capital into and out of the United States, explains Frank Warnock, professor of economics at the Darden Business School at the University of Virginia. Warnock didn't invent the TIC data, but he did work on developing the current incarnation to make what the Treasury publishes more useful to researchers.

This data not only tells us how much capital flowed through America's borders in a given month, but also its various origins and destinations. More specifically, the data tracks cross-border purchases and sales of stocks and bonds, plus cross-border flows of loans and repayments between banks. It doesn't, however, include foreign direct investment, where companies set up or close down factories.

This indicator matters because, in the most simple terms, the more foreigners want to purchase U.S. securities the better it is for everyone in the United States. That's because the rate of interest charged to borrowers is in large part determined by the supply of and demand for debt securities.

Investors pay particularly close attention to how much foreigners are willing to pay to buy U.S. government securities. Such securities are considered risk-free investments and all other borrowers of non-tax-advantaged U.S. dollars pay more to borrow money. If there is a sustained drop-off in demand by foreigners for U.S. government bonds, then it's likely only a matter of time before interest rates rise across the board.

In the early twenty-first century, the big worry of international investors is the fiscal condition of the U.S. government. The federal government borrows in dollars and can make dollars at will, so unlike, say Greece, its technical solvency is not at issue—at least not yet. What investors fret about is the future purchasing power of the dollar, which can drop very quickly indeed, not only at home but especially abroad.

The big question in trying to predict exchange rate movements over the longer term is "whether foreigners are satiated with U.S. securities and, if so, would they then pull out of dollar-denominated assets?" says Warnock.

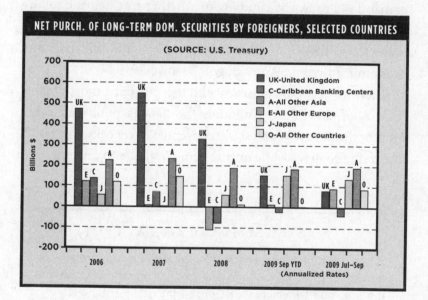

NET PURCH. OF LONG-TERM DOM. SECURITIES BY FOREIGNERS, SELECTED COUNTRIES

(SOURCE: U.S. Treasury)

- UK-United Kingdom
- C-Caribbean Banking Centers
- A-All Other Asia
- E-All Other Europe
- J-Japan
- O-All Other Countries

Investment Strategy

Warnock says looking at the TIC data from the years 2004–5 helped explain a phenomenon that had been puzzling some economists. Specifically, why was it that U.S. interest rates were so low even though there were a number of economic indicators that suggested that interest rates should go higher?

The reason? "Foreigners were buying massive amounts of U.S. treasury bonds," says Warnock. That was driving bond prices higher and interest rates lower. "The TIC data were best suited to capturing that phenomenon."

So when looking at the TIC data, try to figure out whether demand is strong and climbing or whether it's slack and falling by looking at historical flows as well as current ones. If demand looks slack, then it's highly likely interest rates will rise, and economic growth in America will be lower.

There are a couple of issues with the TIC data, most notably its lack of timeliness. Although the data is published every month, the period covered is, on average, six weeks ago. So it's like trying to drive while only looking in the rearview mirror.

EXEC SUMMARY: TIC DATA

When to look: TIC data is released at 9 a.m. ET around the middle of the month for flows taking place a month and a half earlier, (e.g., mid-December for October data).

Where to look: For TIC data, go to *The Wall Street Journal* online's "Market Data Center" at www.WSJMarkets.com. When you are there, you'll need to go to the "Calendars & Economy" section and look under "U.S. Economic Events" for "Treasury International Capital."

Alternatively, you can get TIC data from the U.S. Treasury Department at http://treas.gov/tic/. For TIC-like data for other countries, the IMF (International Monetary Fund) is the place at www.imf.org/external/data.htm.

What to watch for: Increases (decreases) in foreign demand for U.S. securities.

What it means: Pressure on interest rates will be downward (upward).

What steps to take: Watch for additional signs of interest rate movements, and then make appropriate investments, e.g., buying (selling) fixed income funds if rates appear to be heading down (up).

Risk level: Medium.

Profit possibility: $$

MULTIPLE COMPONENTS

MANY ECONOMIC INDICATORS POINT to changes in multiple components of GDP: consumption, investments, government, imports and exports (C, I, G, and NX), which are, after all, just statistical abstractions of very complex and interconnected economic phenomena.

Consumption, for example, is intimately linked to government via taxes—when we consume more, we buy more stuff, which means somebody sold it to us and so that means profits grow and corporate taxes are higher.

Likewise, when banks lend money to businesses, the companies taking on the loans might buy machinery (boosting investment: I) and in turn would likely go out and hire workers to operate those new machines. The workers now employed spend more money (increasing consumption: C) and pay more taxes (helping government: G).

It's not surprising, then, that we include sixteen indicators that point to multiple components of GDP in our Fantastic 50.

BEIGE BOOK
Coincident

THE VERY COLOR BEIGE summons images of institutional mediocrity and bland neutrality. But don't let that deceive you into thinking the Federal Reserve's so-called Beige Book has nothing to say. It does—and how. But unlike many of the other indicators we compiled, the Beige Book does not primarily consist of a series of numbers.

Rather it is a compilation of anecdotes on the state of the U.S. economy. That's right, the Fed actually talks to human beings—specifically businesspeople and economists from each of twelve districts that cover the United States. See the map on page 133 for each district's boundaries.

The final report includes an overall summary of the state of the broad economy. But more importantly it also gives anecdotal detail on each of the twelve geographic districts separately.

It's that granular information that forecasters like reading. The bad news is that means there is a lot to plow through for anyone wanting to use this indicator.

The good news is that the book is only published eight times a year and it's free to anyone with access to the Web. Of course the members of the Fed's policy-making team get it before you do—about two weeks before the scheduled Federal Open Market Committee meetings.

"It gives us a sense of what the Fed governors are reading and for that reason gives insight into their own outlook on the economy," says Joe Brusuelas, an economist at Bloomberg L.P. "It can be useful because it comes out ahead of other data."

Specifically it can help investors work out whether the Fed will increase the cost of borrowing, leave it the same, or lower it. It can also alert smart investors to forthcoming problems.

Sometimes informed people will tell you that the Fed publishes two much more important books: the Blue Book and the Green Book. The problem with those two is that the public can't look at them in a timely manner. That fact makes them very useful for historians but utterly irrelevant for economic forecasting. No matter how good the information in any report, if *you* can't see it, then it's useless.

FEDERAL RESERVE DISTRICTS

(SOURCE: Federal Reserve)

Investment Strategy

Like the other indicators, the Beige Book can be used to help make investment decisions. Check out what the San Francisco district reported in the November 2006 edition:

> Credit quality was high in general with few delinquencies. However, contacts provided scattered reports of delinquencies on loans to home builders, and banks have increased their vigilance over these loans.

Hindsight is twenty-twenty as they say, but the warning signs about the approaching financial crisis that led to the Great Recession were there for those savvy enough to spot them. In that particular case, avoiding investing in housing stocks and mortgage-related investments would have been prudent.

Clearly, events like the recent financial crisis are rare, so finding evidence of impending doom is likely to be relatively uncommon in the pages of this publication. But the Beige Book does still provide nuggets of potential gold to investors.

"Signs of softening in the economy is bullish for bond investors," says Brusuelas. When the Beige Book's anecdotes paint a picture of a weak economy (or at least a weaker than previously thought business environment), then it may be a sign that the Federal Reserve will lower the cost of borrowing by trimming short-term interest rates. That's good for bond investors because the value of bonds increases as interest rates decline, explains Brusuelas.

The same logic applies when the economy is improving. "If the Beige Book says the economy is strong, it probably means interest rates will go up sooner rather than later," says Brusuelas, meaning the Federal Reserve will likely raise the cost to borrow money. It could indicate it's time to avoid bonds, which would decline in value as interest rates rise.

The Beige Book can also be used to gain insight into the strength of different sectors of the economy, such as technology or manufacturing. That's because different industries tend to be concentrated in certain geographic areas. For instance, to see how the technology sector is doing it would be smart to read the section of the report provided by the San Francisco Fed, says Brusuelas. Technology companies are clustered around Silicon Valley in Northern California. If the report shows favorable economic conditions for technology companies, then it might be worth investing in the tech sector of the stock market. By way of example, the

ProShares Ultra Technology exchange-traded fund (ROM) tracks the value of a slew of technology companies. Brusuelas notes that because of its anecdotal nature this indicator should be used in conjunction with other indicators rather than alone.

EXEC SUMMARY: BEIGE BOOK

When to look: At 2 p.m. ET two Wednesdays before the next Federal Open Market Committee meeting. For a schedule of its FOMC meetings, browse: www.federalreserve.gov/fomc/.

Where to look: Reporters and editors of *The Wall Street Journal* read the Beige Book diligently when it is released. Reporters file summary stories as the Fed publishes the report.

A summary is also posted at *The Wall Street Journal* online's "Market Data Center" at WSJMarkets.com. Go to the "Calendars & Economy" section and look under "U.S. Economic Events" for "Beige Book."

Alternatively, you can go directly to the Fed itself at www.federalreserve.gov/FOMC/Beigebook/.

What to watch for: Clues in the report's anecdotes about the overall health of the economy and specific sectors.

What it means: A faceless bureaucrat heard something from the regional business community and considered it important enough to note.

What steps to take: Depends on what the anecdote is, e.g., if the economy appears to be weakening, buy bonds!

Risk level: Varies.

Profit possibility: Varies.

25

CRACK SPREAD
Leading

W E KNOW YOU ARE going to love the crack spread, but not just because you can make lots of construction worker jokes. There are good economic reasons for getting down and dirty with this particular indicator: gasoline.

"The crack spread is an indicator of refinery profitability," says Adam Sieminski, chief energy economist at Deutsche Bank in Washington, D.C. Specifically, it is a measure of the profitability of refining crude oil into gasoline and heating oil. When the crack spread is wide, it's more profitable to refine. When the spread is narrow, it's less profitable. If it were ever to go negative, and stay that way, then refining would actually be a loss-making proposition and we'd likely have no gasoline at the pumps with which to fill our tanks. Still, there'd be plenty of time to read up on other economic indicators instead.

It's called a crack spread because crude oil is said to be cracked, or broken, into other stuff, like gasoline, diesel fuel, heating oil, and lots of other petrochemicals.

The truth is that there are many different crack spreads, but the one investors most care about is the one between crude oil and gasoline. It makes sense. After all, much of our economy runs on gasoline.

The crack spread widens and narrows because the price of gasoline and crude oil do not move in sync. Why? "Because the things that influence the crude oil market and the gasoline market are different," explains Deutsche Bank's Sieminski. "If a refinery shuts down because of a fire or explosion, then heating oil or gasoline prices would likely react but not those of crude oil."

Likewise, announcements from OPEC (Organization of the Petroleum Exporting Countries) likely would affect the price of crude oil but probably wouldn't have an immediate impact on gasoline, he says.

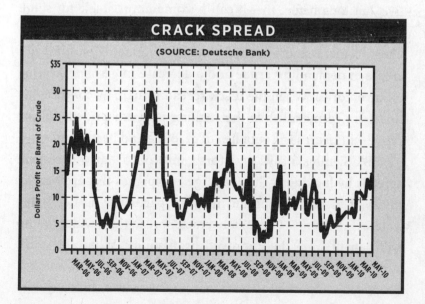

CRACK SPREAD

(SOURCE: Deutsche Bank)

Investment Strategy

The first important thing to note is that crack spreads are seasonal: More gasoline needs to be produced during the spring and summer and more heating oil in the fall and winter. Moreover, during the annual production facility maintenance period—traditionally in late winter—crack spreads rise as fewer refiners are making gasoline. That means the few that are making fuel can charge more.

Many observers believe that total U.S. oil-refinery capacity is below that required during peak periods of demand.

With those caveats always in mind, investors can use the crack spread to predict future supply and demand conditions for fossil fuels. When the crack spread is low, refiners are not making much profit. (The spread only occasionally goes negative, but long before that it can become unprofitable for some high-cost companies to refine oil.) Refiners are therefore not likely to increase production anytime soon, so look for a decrease in demand for crude and a decrease in gasoline/heating oil inventories. When the crack spread is high, by contrast, refiners try to make while the making is good, so demand for crude will rise, as will supplies of gasoline and heating oil.

DB's Sieminski says investors can profit from wider crack spreads by looking at those energy companies that are heavily involved in the refining business. In particular he highlights Valero Energy (VLO). When crack spreads are wide, Valero will benefit from the improved profitability. When the crack spreads are narrow, the firm will likely see its profits diminish, he says. It's important to note that just because a company is in the oil business doesn't mean it is heavily exposed to the refining business. You'll need to do your own research before buying any stock.

Note also that the crack spread provides information about only one side of each market, the demand for crude and the supply of its distillates. Use other indicators, like the Baltic Dirty Tanker Index, to discern the future supply of crude and demand for its distillates and you'll be prepared to profit in those markets and also to better understand the economy's position in the business cycle.

EXEC SUMMARY: CRACK SPREAD

When to look: Continuously for energy prices. Energy trades around the world most business days.

Where to look: Energy prices can be easily obtained in *The Wall Street Journal* online's "Market Data Center." You'll find it at www .WSJMarkets.com. When you are there, you'll need to go to "Commodities & Futures" section and look under "Energy" for "Petroleum." There you will find price data on light crude oil and gasoline. That's just the first step. After you have the prices of the near-term contracts, you'll need to do some math. Calculating the crack spread is a little tricky, though. Crude oil prices are quoted by the barrel, while gasoline and heating oil are quoted by the gallon. (There are forty-two gallons in a barrel.) There is also the question of weighting. Traditionally, three barrels of crude will produce two of gasoline and one of heating oil, but other combinations are possible. Using the traditional 3–2–1 method, the crack spread equation is:

(84 * gasoline price + 42 * heating oil price—3 * crude price)/3.

Alternatively, the New York Mercantile Exchange division of the

CME Group provides a handy calculator at www.nymex.com/calc_crack.aspx/.

To get regular historical charts of crack spreads, you'll likely have to subscribe to a fee-based data service.

What to watch for: Higher (lower) crack spreads.

What it means: Refining oil into gasoline is more (less) profitable.

What steps to take: Buy (sell) refinery-heavy stocks like Valero.

Risk level: High.

Profit possibility: $$$

26

CREDIT AVAILABILITY OSCILLATOR
Leading

(*See also* Libor)

THE FILM *CABARET*'s famous song "Money, Money" gets it almost right when it says "Money makes the world go around." The truth is that for businesses and the economy it's credit, or borrowed money, that really keeps things going.

The world found out exactly how much credit keeps things going when it all dried up in the fall of 2008 during the Great Credit Crunch, which quickly went on to become the Great Recession.

If the credit crisis of 2008 taught the world anything, it's that without the free flow of borrowed money, the world of business quickly comes to a standstill, and with that so does the economy.

Broadly speaking, when loans are more available to both businesses and individuals, more economic activity occurs and the economy expands. When loans are hard to come by, you can expect business activity to slow down and the economy to falter.

That was the idea in mind in 2007 when some savvy bond market analysts at Philadelphia investment bank Janney Montgomery Scott developed the Credit Availability Oscillator. That their work predated the credit crisis only shows how prescient they were.

Guy LeBas, head of fixed income strategy at Janney and a key architect of the CAO, says he was keenly aware of the economy's dependence on credit.

"Borrowing availability is a huge part of consumer spending," says LeBas. In 2007 he was particularly worried about what would happen to spending if homeowners couldn't refinance their mortgages. That's why he developed the CAO, which is pronounced "cow." No joke.

Although Janney keeps the CAO's exact internal workings top secret, LeBas does detail some of the many metrics used, which include both qualitative and quantitative inputs. They are all focused on determining how easy or hard it is to borrow money.

A survey of qualitative data is collected quarterly on the difficulty of obtaining different types of loans. That quarterly data is supplemented with daily quantitative inputs. (Those inputs should be called moos—moos in the cao. Geddit!) The result is a daily CAO reading.

The quant data includes the prices at which certain types of bonds are trading, particularly those involving automobile loans made to consumers as well as borrowing by people with a less than stellar credit history, so-called subprime borrowers. Also included are the interest rates at which banks lend to each other, the Libor rate, a key measure of how well credit is flowing between lending institutions.

Although the CAO was only developed in 2007, Janney has developed historical data to provide context, as shown in the following chart.

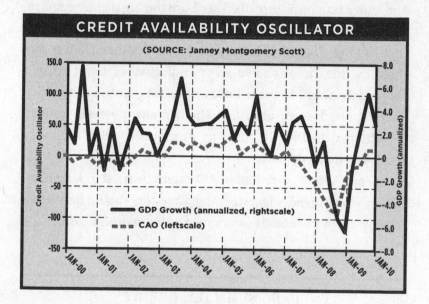

Investment Strategy

Unlike some other economic indicators, the CAO is relatively easy to understand. Zero indicates a neutral level of credit availability. It tells you that it's neither very easy nor very hard to obtain a loan. A positive reading says credit is flowing relatively freely. In the mid–2000s, the indicator registered in the 20s and 30s, but in late 2006 the index plunged and turned negative for the first time since 2002.

"It was telling us that lending conditions were rapidly deteriorating," says LeBas. "The implications are very broad because it suggests weaker corporate profitability, lower demand, and softer economic growth. Those are the big picture implications."

CAO data that includes qualitative survey data from two or three quarters is of course more indicative of trends than a single data point. Because LeBas has access to the component data inputs, he can also see whether any possible trend is broadly matched by the majority of inputs or whether it's the result of a data anomaly.

Special note: A very high CAO might be used to help identify an asset bubble, suggesting that investors should deleverage (or pay down their loans) and move investments to cash.

EXEC SUMMARY: CREDIT AVAILABILITY OSCILLATOR

When to look: When your Janney Montgomery Scott research report arrives.

Where to look: The CAO is a proprietary index of Janney Montgomery Scott. That's good news if you are a client of Janney's. LeBas says information on the CAO is provided to the firm's clients through its published research.

If you're not a Janney client, then following the CAO will be more tricky, but not impossible. Research reports of all the major banks have typically managed to find their way across the Web. So scouring the Internet might be a useful start. In addition, this sort of indicator tends to get followed by the press especially when there are marked changes in the levels. That's precisely the time you'd want to hear about it.

What to watch for: The CAO moving up (down).

What it means: Borrowing is easier (harder) so the economy will likely grow (shrink) in the near term.

What steps to take: Looks like a good time (really stinky time) to go for broke in the stock market.

Risk level: Medium.

Profit possibility: $$

27

FEDERAL FUNDS RATE
Leading

(*See also* Libor, Ted Spread, Credit Spreads, Yield Curve)

WHEN YOU DRIVE A car, you step on the gas pedal to make it go faster and the brake to slow things down. Well, the Federal Reserve, the U.S. central bank, has a similar gadget for the economy. If the Fed wants to slow down the economy, it raises its so-called Fed funds interest rate, the rate at which banks lend to each other overnight. If it wants to speed up the economy, it lowers the rate.

Of course driving the economy this way is a bit trickier than driving a car. The Fed funds rate is a target set by the Fed's Federal Open Market Committee (FOMC). It's effective because the rate directly affects other interest rates, including mortgage payments for adjustable-rate mortgages (so-called ARMs), credit card rates, and the interest that banks pay to customers on their savings accounts, explains Ellen Zentner, a New York–based economist at the Bank of Tokyo-Mitsubishi.

"When the FOMC changes the rate, it changes the cost of doing business for the bank," says Zentner. "When those costs are raised, they are immediately passed on to the consumers."

So if the Fed raises rates it has a quick impact of increasing the cost of consumer loans and credit card debt. That leaves people with less money to spend on goods and services. For that reason, the economy will tend to slow down—or at least growth will moderate—when the Fed funds rate is hiked.

Although the FOMC tends to raise rates in small increments, it can have a big impact on some people. "A tiny change in the Fed funds rate could represent the straw that breaks the camel's back for any household that is burdened with debt," explains Zentner. Likewise, a drop in the Fed funds rate can be manna from heaven for people deep in credit card debt, as it lowers their monthly payments.

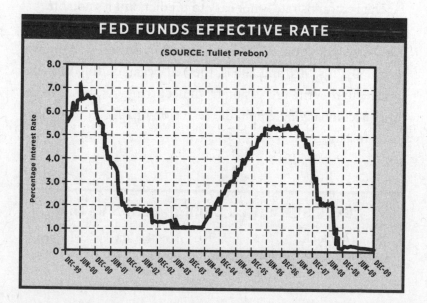

FED FUNDS EFFECTIVE RATE

(SOURCE: Tullet Prebon)

Investment Strategy

The Fed funds rate is so closely watched that other business at the big banks can come to a halt when the FOMC is expected to make a decision on whether to change interest rates.

The value of stocks and bonds is determined in part by interest rates. In general, lower Fed funds rates mean bonds are worth more. Stocks can also be worth more when rates are low because it means the cost of borrowing is lower, meaning more money is left for profits and less paid to the bank.

For that reason, sometimes unexpectedly bad economic data on jobs, manufacturing, and so forth can actually cause bond and equity markets to move *higher* by increasing expectations that the Fed will cut its target rate or at least leave it unchanged.

The Fed funds rate is not easy to predict. But it's notable that not a single recession since World War II has ended without a good-size reduction in Fed funds rate. On several occasions in the 1960s, 70s, 90s, and 2000s, the Fed began cutting rates but too late to prevent a recession from occurring. As shown in the other accompanying graph, the recession of 2008–9 was one of those instances.

EXEC SUMMARY: FEDERAL FUNDS RATE

When to look: At 2:15 p.m. ET on days that the Federal Open Market Committee meets, which is at least every six weeks. For a schedule, browse: www.federalreserve.gov/fomc/.

Where to look: Go to *The Wall Street Journal* online's "Market Data Center" at www.WSJMarkets.com. Look under "Bonds, Rates & Credit Markets" tab for "Consumer Money Rates" and find the "Fed Funds" target rate.

The St. Louis Fed's FRED database is another favorite source for historical data on the Fed funds target (and all other interest rates and lots more besides). Any number of news outlets will post the FOMC's most recent announcement within seconds of its release.

For expectations about future Fed funds rate changes, see the federal funds futures. How Fed funds futures work is nicely described by the Cleveland Fed at www.clevelandfed.org/research/data/fedfunds/.

What to watch for: Increases (decreases) in the federal funds target rate.

What it means: The economy is likely to slow down (speed up) in the coming months.

What steps to take: Start selling (buying) manufacturing stocks. Also think about which companies are going to make it through the coming economic storm relatively unscathed.

Risk level: Low.

Profit possibility: $

28.

FERTILITY RATES
Leading

I F SEX DOESN'T MAKE the world go round, it comes pretty close. That's because births of people—the frequent result of having sex—drives spending patterns for decades afterward.

The idea here is that people as a group tend to follow distinct patterns of activity depending on their age. For instance, Americans typically get married and have children in their late twenties. At the same time they tend to buy houses. Later the children grow up, leave home, and then the parents save to get ready for retirement.

However, each generation isn't uniform in size. After World War II, a huge spurt in births in the United States—the baby boom—created a demographic bulge that has driven many trends in the latter half of the twentieth century and the first part of the twenty-first century.

"The baby boom generation has raised their families, has started saving their money, and now they are beginning to retire," says Harry S. Dent Jr., author of *The Great Depression Ahead* (2009). Dent has studied birth trends—also known as the fertility rate in the jargon of demographers—and what's particularly noticeable is that the generation born immediately following the boomers, generation X, is much smaller in size.

Because these generations differ in size, the way that overall income will be divided among different areas of the economy will change radically over time. For instance, the portion of income spent on health care is set to increase as the baby boomers age. This study of likely overall spending patterns gives economists and investors alike a glimpse of the future.

The other thing we know about fertility rates is that they go down as countries get richer. Or more simply, women in the richer nations of the world tend to have fewer babies. The theory behind this is that there is less economic incentive to have children in richer countries.

For instance, in poor countries children can be put to work to help make ends meet. Also when people grow old, more children are available to look after their parents, if necessary. Those things are less of an issue in the richer states of the world where to some extent laws prevent children from being put to work and where governments typically provide a social safety net for the elderly.

Thus economies where people are getting richer will see smaller families and more discretionary income for spending on things like education, automobiles, and houses.

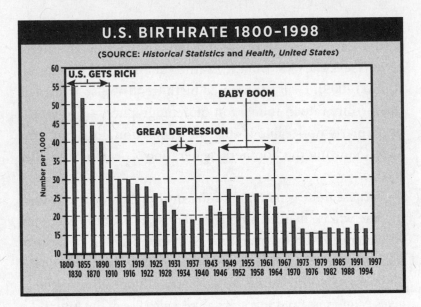

U.S. BIRTHRATE 1800-1998

(SOURCE: *Historical Statistics* and *Health, United States*)

Investment Strategy

Fertility rates have some serious implications for investors, especially when it comes to asset allocation. For example, Dent points out that the demographics look positive for the U.S. health care industry, so those stocks may be worth a look for investors willing to take a risk. The reasoning works as follows: Most people spend *more* on health care as they age. The baby boomers are no different, but because there are proportionately so many more boomers than there are people in other generations in the United States, health care businesses will need to grow faster than the overall economy in order to keep up with demand.

The publicly traded health care stocks will in all likelihood benefit from this trend. For that reason, demographics suggest that investors might want to consider overweighting their asset allocation toward health care stocks. As usual there are many factors at play, so savvy investors should do their own research before making any decisions.

Dent also sees the demographic bulge caused by the baby boom leading to an increase in the overall savings rate. The thinking behind this is clear: As people head closer to retirement, they tend to save more. This is nothing new; the parents of the boomers did the same. And if there were not a demographic bulge, this fact would have no economic impact. If that were the case, increased saving by the boomer generation would be offset by more spending by the subsequent cohort, generation X.

But there *is* a demographic bulge, so spending by generation X will not fill the void created by boomers increasing their saving.

Dent sees the increase in savings as detrimental to the U.S. economy. High savings, in his view, will mean lower growth for a considerable period and a sluggish stock market for about a decade—through about 2020 he says.

In our view the net increase in savings also means more money will be available for investment. Economists are forever telling people that savings must equal investment when looked at in the aggregate.

It's true that the money being invested won't flow to the same places as it would if it was spent for consumption. But it will go somewhere, and the trick is to follow where that investment money is going. To do so, you'll need to use the other economic indicators. In particular, check out durable goods orders to see if there is growth in machinery investment.

EXEC SUMMARY: FERTILITY RATES

When to look: The lags on birth data are long and variable depending on the country. So grab recent data whenever you can.

Where to look: For the United States up to 1998, use Historical Statistics, as we did above. For more recent data, see the National Center for Health Statistics at www.cdc.gov/nchs/, especially the annual report Health, United States. For data on other nations, go to NationMaster.com at www.nationmaster.com/graph/peo_bir_rat-people-birth-rate. Or check out the CIA World Factbook at www.cia.gov/library/publications/the-world-factbook/rankorder/2054rank.html.

You can also look at Harry Dent's book, *The Great Depression Ahead: How to Prosper in the Crash Following the Greatest Boom in History*. We don't necessarily buy all the ideas he promotes, but he does show how birthrate data can be used to help investors make allocation decisions.

What to watch for: Demographic changes, especially fertility rates.

What it means: Future changes in aggregate demand and the demand for specific goods and services, such as education and health care.

What steps to take: Buy health care stocks while the boomers age and still have the money to pay. Buy higher education stocks when small bulges are due to enter college.

Risk level: High.

Profit possibility: $$$

29

GROSS DOMESTIC PRODUCT (GDP) PER CAPITA
Coincident

How DO WE KNOW if we are getting richer? Per capita GDP is one of the best ways to answer that question. Or put another way, how much does the average person earn/produce in a country? The higher per capita GDP is the richer the people in that country are, on average. Despite its obvious importance, this indicator receives surprisingly little explanation. Here's an example: For the first time in over a century, China's economy is projected to be bigger than that of Japan in 2010. Does that mean the Chinese people are on average richer than the Japanese? *Yomi no!* (*Yomi* is the Shinto word for hell, by the way.) China's slightly higher total income is divided among many, many more people.

The official estimates from the CIA show both countries with economies of about $5 trillion in 2009. But here's the rub:

Japan has only 130 million people to China's 1.3 billion. So GDP per capita in Japan was about ten times that of China.

"In the same way a doctor listens to the heartbeat of a patient to determine their basic health, an economist looks at the per capita GDP to understand the health of the economy," says Robert Dye, senior economist at the PNC Financial Services Group in Pittsburgh. "A high per capita GDP country will have a more developed economy."

Dye says that per capita GDP is one of the key determinants of standard of living. In general, people who live in countries with high per capita GDP tend to have higher standards of living.

An important caveat, he says, is the distribution of income. Is income widely distributed with most people earning close to the average? Or is income concentrated in the hands of an elite few who have massive incomes while the rest of the populace scrapes by? Clearly, those two scenarios aren't comparable.

The best way to measure equality is the Gini coefficient. At zero, all incomes are exactly equal. At 1 (or 100), one dude has it all and everyone else nothing. Neither has ever been observed, not even in communist countries or Saddam Hussein's Iraq. Many countries with Gini coefficients between .15 and .45— pretty equal incomes—exist. That is important because countries with widely dispersed incomes (lower Gini scores) are more politically stable and also are better for business relative to those where income is concentrated in the hands of a few.

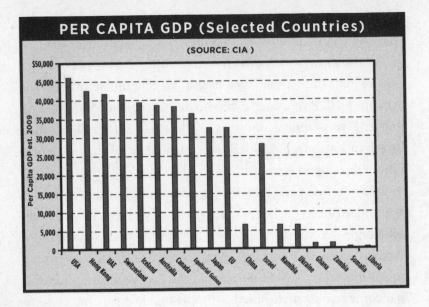

Investment Strategy

As countries get richer, the people in those countries can start to afford more than just the basic necessities. "When you live on a dollar a day, then you can't afford much more than food," says Dye. "But as you get richer you can start spending on luxuries."

At that level, we're probably talking about shoes, clothes, and lightbulbs. Still, that's how progress starts, one convenience or comfort at a time. Countries beginning to surf up the "rich" scale can provide good markets for new products for a growing consumer culture.

Again, there are caveats: Check out the legal structure in

those countries. In general, a good legal structure for businesses protects property rights and ensures minimal corruption.

Countries at the bottom of the per capita GDP ladder typically engage in low value-added agriculture and low value-added manufacturing. To get up the ladder they need to start engaging in higher value-added businesses. Watch for countries that are using government policy to drive that development process as potentially fast-growing economies. Chile in the 1970s is a great example as is South Korea in the 1960s through the 1990s.

In general, investors like to invest in fast-growing economies with friendly legal systems. As with anything, the potential for high rewards comes hand in hand with big risks. So to mitigate the risk of investing directly in so-called emerging economies, typically through local stocks, it can make sense to pick sophisticated companies that are doing business in those places. U.S.-based multinational corporations are a good place to start.

EXEC SUMMARY: GROSS DOMESTIC PRODUCT (GDP) PER CAPITA

When to look: The first estimates for GDP come out at 8:30 a.m. ET the final week of January, April, July, and October. A month later a revision is released and a month after that a second revision. So near the end of every month you'll find some sort of an estimate of GDP.

Where to look: Editors and writers at *The Wall Street Journal* watch GDP data closely. As news about it is released, *Journal* reporters file breaking news stories for publication on WSJ.com.

Alternatively, MeasuringWorth.com has annual data for America and the United Kingdom. For other countries see NationMaster .com or the CIA *World Factbook* at www.CIA.gov. The OECD provides data at www.OECD.org, and the World Bank websites at www.worldbank.org are also good sources for other countries.

What to watch for: Increases in real per capita GDP, a low or declining level of income inequality, and a tolerable administration of justice.

What it means: Rapid economic development may be in the offing.

What steps to take: Take equity stakes in multinational enterprises with heavy exposure to the emerging market or, for the risk loving, its domestic companies. Multinational enterprises are those companies with extensive operations across the globe—think Pepsi, General Motors, and Caterpillar as examples.

Risk level: Medium to astronomical.

Profit possibility: $$ to $$$$

30

LIBOR
Leading

(*See also* Credit Availability Oscillator, Ted Spread)

Y OU MIGHT FEEL THAT sometimes the bank doesn't trust you. Well, if you think that's bad, get this: Sometimes they don't even trust each other.

We can measure trust (or the lack thereof) by looking at the interest rate banks charge each other for short-term, unsecured loans—meaning there is nothing backing up the loans other than the good faith and creditworthiness of the borrowing bank.

The cost in percentage terms for a bank to borrow money under such terms is known as the Libor, or the London Interbank Offered Rate, and it's published daily by the British Bankers' Association (BBA).

Ashraf Laidi, chief market strategist at CMC Markets in London, says rising Libor rates reflect a decline in the availability of funds and stresses in the overall financial system. Or more simply, when Libor rises, money isn't flowing as freely between the banks. "When the Libor is being reset in London at eleven a.m., that is partially a pulse of liquidity amongst banks," he says.

Libor is calculated for ten different currencies, including the American, Australian, Canadian, and New Zealand dollars, British pounds sterling, Swiss francs, Japanese yen, Danish krones, and Swedish kronas. The rates are also set for varying lengths of loans, from as short as overnight through as long as twelve months. In short, it's a lot of numbers.

Official Libor data goes back to 1986 when the BBA helped to standardize the measurement of these rates. That was particularly important at the time due to the introduction of a then-newfangled derivative product known as an interest rate swap.

Libor has implications far beyond just what banks think of each other. That's because Libor is the basis for how much interest is charged for many adjustable-rate loans made to consumers and other businesses, including floating-rate mortgages.

That alone makes Libor important because housing costs usually represent the biggest monthly expense for most consumers. When mortgage costs jump, people have less money to spend on other things and at worst can leave people unable to pay their mortgages, and we don't have to tell you that can spell big trouble.

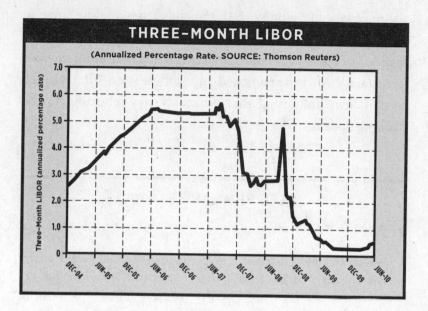

THREE-MONTH LIBOR

(Annualized Percentage Rate. SOURCE: Thomson Reuters)

Investment Strategy

For the most part, Libor does what interest rates normally do—fall during recessions and rise during booms. The economics of this is simple: Demand by consumers and businesses to borrow money chases up interest rates during the economic good times. The opposite occurs during an economic slump—fewer people want to borrow less money so interest rates fall back.

Libor is particularly insightful during financial crises. It dropped leading into the recession of 2008 as we would expect, but then it spiked during the financial crisis that fall, as the so-called credit crunch took hold.

Laidi says that spikes in rates, just like the one in 2008, were a sign of lack of liquidity in the financial system. The spike in rates also represented a risk premium, a large payment demanded of those with money to lend during periods of massive uncertainty. After the panicked atmosphere subsided, Libor fell to new lows, indicating that normalcy was returning to the banking system.

EXEC SUMMARY: LIBOR

When to look: Daily.

Where to look: Libor data is easily found in *The Wall Street Journal* online's "Market Data Center" at www.WSJMarkets.com. When you are there, you'll need to go to the "Bonds, Rates & Credit Markets" tab and look under "Consumer Money Rates" for Libor.

Alternatively, the British Bankers' Association has set up a website specifically for the purpose of providing information on Libor, www.bbalibor.com, where you can download current and historic data on Libor rates in different currencies. It also has a Twitter feed: twitter.com/BBALIBOR. Note that the BBA stresses the data is for personal use, not for businesses. That may be good enough for your purposes.

Another avenue worth pursuing: Libor data is available from Economagic.com at www.economagic.com/libor.htm.

What to watch for: Increases (decreases) in Libor rates.

What it means: The economy is heating up (cooling down) or banks are demanding a high-risk premium due to uncertainty.

What steps to take: Take appropriate cyclical action if the change appears linked to the business cycle; scramble for cash if a spike is due to panic.

Risk level: Medium.

Profit possibility: $$

31

M2 MONEY SUPPLY
Leading

(*See also* Credit Spreads)

M2 IS A MEASURE of how much money there is in the economy. It is relatively easy for you and me to determine how much money we have (or don't have), but it's much harder to know the same for the overall economy. That's because for economists "money" is a nebulous term. It's not just bills and coins, but also can include bank accounts. And there's where it starts to get tricky because there are moneylike accounts that work just like bank accounts at places that aren't banks and some bank accounts that can't be included for one reason or another.

So economists came up with different measures of money, from very narrow (M0) to very broad (M3) ones. M2 is a broad measure of how much money is in the economy, and it includes paper bills (notes) and coins as well as checking and savings accounts. Not all bank account balances are included, only those worth less than $100,000. Also, some non–bank accounts, like retail money market mutual funds, are included.

The Federal Reserve can influence the size of M2 because it has the ability to create money out of nothing and to return it to that same nothingness. The Fed performs this money magic by buying or selling U.S. government debt, or similar financial instruments. When the Fed sells Treasuries, it does so for cash and by doing so it takes that cash out of the economy and reduces the money supply. When the Fed buys Treasuries, it uses cash to make the purchase. Or in other words it pumps money into the economy, expanding the money supply, including M2.

Typically, the Fed deliberately increases M2 to speed up the economy. It decreases M2 to slow the economy. But it's not just the Fed that determines how much money is in the economy. Commercial banks, like Wells Fargo and the Bank of America, can create or destroy money, specifically deposits, as well. They do so by making loans and crediting the borrowers' checking accounts. During an economic expansion, when the economy is growing, bankers make loans more freely. In recessions they are stricter about making loans, leading to the adage that a banker gives you an umbrella when the sun is shining, but takes it away once it rains.

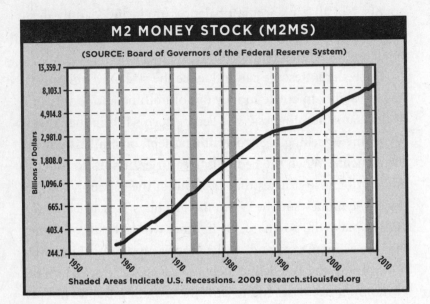

M2 MONEY STOCK (M2MS)

(SOURCE: Board of Governors of the Federal Reserve System)

Shaded Areas Indicate U.S. Recessions. 2009 research.stlouisfed.org

Investment Strategy

M2 can help forecast whether the economy is about to exit a recession or enter one. It's not foolproof, but if used carefully you can get an idea of what is going on sooner than by waiting to see GDP data. By then the turning point is long gone.

The theory is that the economy grows when the M2 growth rate increases but contracts when M2 declines. For example, the U.S. economy was in recession from March until November 2001. The data shows that the annual rate of M2 growth slowed considerably in 1999, and in 2000 it remained below the 1997–99 average. M2 leapt in 2001, during the recession, predating the actual recovery.

For an investor that's really useful to know because it tells you what is going to happen ahead of time. This foresight gives you time to change your investments to those areas that do well early in a recovery, which historically have been growth stocks and small companies. However, it's not foolproof. "[T]he growth rate of broad money [is] an imperfect proxy for nominal demand [or GDP]," wrote Michael Darda, director of research at Greenwich-based trading firm MKM Partners, in a research report in 2010.

Why? Because the speed at which money moves around the economy, the so-called velocity of money, sometimes varies. Economists believe that slow-moving money has less economic impact than fast-moving money. Further to this point, Darda observes that the recovery of the early 1990s and the second leg of the Great Depression in 1937 saw a drop in money velocity, making M2 growth less reliable as an indicator.

He does note, however, that there was a very tight relationship between M2 and GDP growth from 1960 to 1989. A rule of thumb is that as the cost of corporations borrowing money declines—relative to that of government borrowing (the so-called credit spread)—the velocity of money increases.

EXEC SUMMARY: M2 MONEY SUPPLY

When to look: Every Thursday at 4:30 p.m. ET for data from two weeks prior.

Where to look: For the data go to *The Wall Street Journal* online's

"Market Data Center" at www.WSJMarkets.com. You'll need to go to the "Calendars & Economy" section and look under "U.S. Economic Events" for "Money Supply."

Alternative sources include the Federal Reserve's main website and the FRED database at the St. Louis Fed.

What to watch for: Increases (decreases) in M2.

What it means: The economy is heating up (maybe cooling down).

What steps to take: Get into stocks (liquid assets such as cash) because the economy may be improving (deteriorating).

Risk level: Medium.

Profit possibility: $$

32

NEW HOME SALES
Leading

(*See also* Existing Home Sales, Housing Starts, and Pending Home Sales)

THE AMERICAN DREAM FOR many is to own their own home. But for a lucky few it goes further: Their dream is buying a brand new house that no one has lived in before.

Sales of new homes aren't the largest part of the housing market, but they are a good leading indicator of future economic activity, explains Mike Larson, a real estate analyst at Jupiter, Florida–based boutique Weiss Research.

New homes normally account for around 15–25% of total home sales with the remainder made up of existing or pre-owned homes, he says. He points out that in the wake of the popping of the real estate bubble, that number had fallen closer to 5% in 2010, but he expects it to rebound to the norm at some point.

New home sales act as a leading indicator because new

houses are frequently purchased before they are built. Unlike with existing home sales, the new home sales data measures when contracts are signed, not when the keys are handed over to the new owners.

News that thousands of new homes were sold in a given month says that there will be future economic activity as the houses actually get built. Workers need to be hired, and lumber, floor tiles, roofing materials, and electrical wiring, to name just a few things, must be manufactured, transported, and warehoused before finally being used at the actual construction site.

All of that activity shows up as increased GDP. So rising levels of new home sales tend to foreshadow better economic times. Likewise, consistently falling sales of new homes tend to portend a weakening economy.

Any type of home—condo, loft, or house—is a major purchase that many people need to borrow to make. To do so, buyers need to have confidence in their ability to hold down a job and that any other sources of income are reasonably secure. Typically, that means that strong home sales, new and existing, go hand in hand with a robust jobs market.

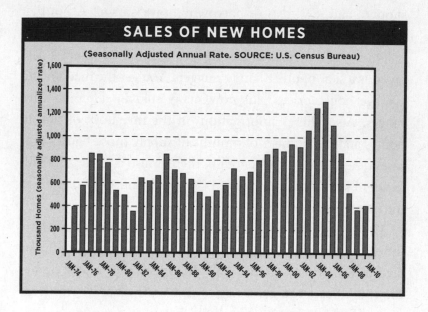

SALES OF NEW HOMES

(Seasonally Adjusted Annual Rate. SOURCE: U.S. Census Bureau)

Investment Strategy

The claim that strong and rising new home sales actually augur better economic times is borne out in the accompanying chart. If you look closely, you'll see that new home sales typically turn down just before recessions strike and move upward before the recovery of the overall economy begins.

The data can also be used to see where the housing market is heading.

Ideally, what you want to see in the new home sales data, which is provided each month by the Census Bureau, are affordable prices, low inventory levels (represented in months of supply), and low costs of borrowing, says Larson. All of that could point to good growth in home sales ahead.

On top of annualized sales figures, the new home sales data gives us a slew of other handy nuggets. You get the median and average house prices plus how many sold in different price ranges. Also, there's information on the inventory of unsold homes and the number of months of supply those figures represent. As if that weren't enough, there is also a regional breakdown of sales. Larson points to the South and West regions as the most important.

Using all of that data together with the knowledge of where different home-building companies operate (the geographic area in which they operate and the price range of the homes they build) can be a good way to decide whether it's worth investing in the different home-builder stocks.

Alternatively, for those not wanting to invest in specific stocks, investors might want to consider looking at the SPDR S&P Homebuilders (XHB) exchange-traded fund, which tracks a basket of home builders.

"Strong new home sales data would be good for cabinetmakers, tile makers, home builders, manufacturers of faucets, and those selling raw wood products like Weyerhauser," says Larson.

EXEC SUMMARY: NEW HOME SALES

When to look: Monthly data is made available at 10:00 a.m. ET about four weeks after the fact. That's around the 25th day of the month.

Where to look: Editors and writers at *The Wall Street Journal* watch home sales data closely. As news about it and capacity utilization is released, Journal reporters file breaking news stories for publication on WSJ.com.

If it's just the data that you want, go to *The Wall Street Journal* online's "Market Data Center" at www.WSJMarkets.com. When you are there, you'll need to go to the "Calendars & Economy" section and look under "U.S. Economic Events" for "New Home Sales." New home sales can also be tracked through the Census Bureau, at www.census.gov/newhomesales.

What to watch for: Increases (decreases) in new housing starts.

What it means: The economy is heating up (cooling down).

What steps to take: Purchase (sell) home-builder stocks or ETFs and the shares of companies that supply home materials like lumber.

Risk level: Medium to high.

Profit possibility: $$ to $$$

33

PHILADELPHIA FED: THE ARUOBA-DIEBOLD-SCOTTI BUSINESS CONDITIONS INDEX

Coincident

(*See also* Weekly Leading Index, Philadelphia Fed: Business Outlook Survey)

PHILADELPHIA SHOWS ITSELF TO be truly the city of brotherly love by giving investors some special kindness: a slew of economic indicators, published by the Philadelphia Federal Reserve, part of America's mighty central bank.

Unlike men, which the Declaration of Independence says are all created equal, one indicator from Philly stands out above the rest: the Aruoba-Diebold-Scotti Business Conditions Index. That's a mouthful to pronounce (and spell), but you don't need to say (or spell) it to use it. We'll call it ADS here to save you and this book's copy editors any further consternation.

This index takes in a variety of economic data, mashes it all together, and comes out with an up-to-the-minute reading on the economy with a frequency of at least once a week. It saves common investors like you and me a lot of hard work trying to grapple with the individual pieces.

The input data includes a composite of quarterly output data, unemployment indicators, industrial production, personal income less transfer payments, and manufacturing/trade sales, plus GDP growth.

"What the ADS does is aggregate all this data in a statistically meaningful manner," says Keith Sill, director of real-time data research at the Federal Reserve Bank of Philadelphia.

The economic whizzes at the Philly Fed use a filter to help smooth the data so that the impact of less frequent data, like the GDP growth figures, blends seamlessly with those of more frequent indicators, like weekly new claims for unemployment insurance.

Unlike the other Philly Fed indicator discussed in this book, the Business Outlook Survey, the ADS looks at the entire economy, not just the Philly Fed's rather tiny district. Additionally, because the ADS is updated so frequently—at least once a week and sometimes more frequently—it's a real-time read on the economy that analysts don't have to wait a long time for, unlike the quarterly read on GDP.

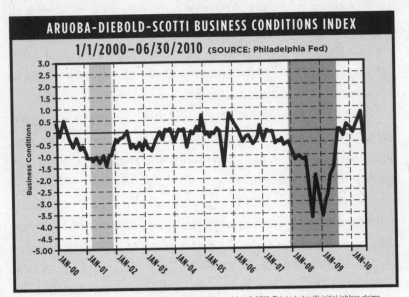

ARUOBA-DIEBOLD-SCOTTI BUSINESS CONDITIONS INDEX

1/1/2000–06/30/2010 (SOURCE: Philadelphia Fed)

Note: We construct the ADS Index using the latest data available as of July 2, 2010. This includes (1) initial jobless claims through the week ending June 26, 2010, (2) payroll employment through June 2010, (3) industrial production through May 2010, (4) real personal income through May 2010, (5) real manufacturing and trade sales through April 2010, and (6) real GDP through the first quarter of 2010. Lighter gray shading indicates historical NBER-designated recessions. Darker gray shading indicates the recent recession, designated by the NBER to have started in December 2007 but not yet designated by the NBER to have ended (as of the date of creation of this figure). We end it in July 2009, which appears likely conditional on information presently available, but we use darker gray as a reminder that our dating is not official.

Investment Strategy

Reading the ADS is easy. The average value is zero. Higher than zero is a plus for the economy. Negative figures are seen as downers, economically speaking.

The ADS index may be used to compare business conditions at different times. A value of –3.0, for example, would indicate business conditions significantly worse than at any time in either the 1990–91 or the 2001 recession, during which the ADS index never dropped below –2.0.

Now there are a couple of wrinkles with this indicator. The zero average gets recalibrated periodically. What that means in practice is that all the historical ADS data you have needs to be jettisoned periodically and the new recalibrated numbers used.

Sills says the best way to look at a reading is to compare a given ADS level to that of some point in the past with a similar reading. Because the data is estimated all the way back to 1960, there are many business cycles to look at and compare.

Fortunately for the budding economic forecaster, the Philly Fed puts out a time series chart of the ADS with bars indicating recessions. This enables investors to easily compare the readings of the ADS going into and out of past recessions.

EXEC SUMMARY: PHILADELPHIA FED: THE ARUOBA-DIEBOLD-SCOTTI BUSINESS CONDITIONS INDEX

When to look: Daily.

Where to look: Data and other resources on the ADS Business Conditions Index are available for free at the Philly Fed's Real-Time Data Research Center at www.phil.frb.org/research-and-data/real-time-center/. The data is "updated as data on the index's underlying components are released."

What to watch for: Increases (decreases) in ADS.

What it means: The economy is heating up (cooling down).

What steps to take: Get into (out of) riskier assets like stocks or high yield/junk bonds.

Risk level: Medium.

Profit possibility: $$

34

PHILADELPHIA FED: BUSINESS OUTLOOK SURVEY
Leading

(*See also* Philadelphia Fed:
The Aruoba-Diebold-Scotti Business Conditions Index)

IMAGINE A RATHER PLAIN-LOOKING unopened tub of ice cream. Now imagine when opened it was jammed full of all the goodies you know you love, like pecans and caramel, plus some more nibbles you never tasted before but now love even more than your previous favorites.

That's the way to think about the Philadelphia Federal Reserve's Business Outlook Survey. For people who want to get into the weeds at the most granular level possible, this is a must-read indicator, the closest thing to Japan's Tankan Survey available in America. (The Philly Fed also publishes the Aruoba-Diebold-Scotti Business Conditions Index, which savvy investors should keep a close eye on also.)

On the surface the BOS can look rather drab. It is after all a survey about manufacturing in just one small area of the economy, eastern Pennsylvania, southern New Jersey, and all of Delaware. But don't let that fool you into dismissing it as irrelevant.

Its first beauty is simplicity in the metric itself, the "diffusion index." That's the metric that measures how the survey participants—manufacturers in the district—feel about a given topic. The headline index measures answers to the question: "What is your evaluation of the level of general business activity?" However, the survey asks not only how the economy is now, but also how good or bad will it be in six months. A number over zero indicates an expansion, or growth in the manufacturing subsector of the economy. A number below zero indicates a contraction.

Now here comes the really good stuff. On top of the overall diffusion index, there are a slew of subtopics on very specific parts of the business world: new orders, shipments, unfilled orders, delivery times, inventories, prices paid, prices received, number of employees, average workweek, and capital expenditures.

"What component I am most interested in is somewhat dependent on where we are in the business cycle," explains Tim Quinlan, a Charlotte-based economist at banking powerhouse Wells Fargo.

For instance, in the early stages of a recovery Quinlan looks at the employment figures. Before hiring starts to get going, the hours worked start to increase. Quinlan says business owners have the attitude that "I will gradually call people back to work, but only once I have my full-time staff back working as many hours as they can."

That means sustained increases in hours worked can be an

important leading indicator, or one that moves ahead of the overall economy.

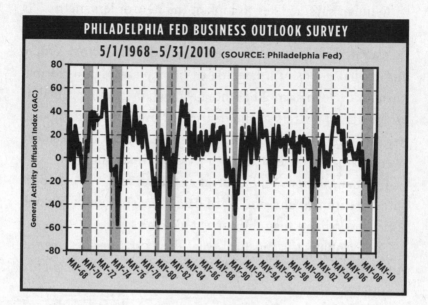

Investment Strategy

While the absolute level of the diffusion index is important, the readings need to be used in conjunction with the change in the level from the previous period. For instance, a drop in the indicator from very positive (like 26) to only slightly positive (maybe 3) is a worrying sign.

Likewise, a move from very negative (–30) to only slightly negative (–5) can look positive, especially if it signals a turning point in the economy.

The other trick with this indicator is to dig into the subindexes and look at which stocks might do well if the particular index changes.

Quinlan says he likes to look at the new orders metric. "Is that increasing or not? If it is, then I would expect to see a commensurate rise in business spending and then factory orders and capital goods at a later date," he explains. "In a normal business cycle that would eventually mean increased profitability for manufacturers in the district." If other indicators point in a similar direction it might make sense to track down stocks of companies in the district with a view to investing.

Quinlan cautions that as great as the survey is, it is a measure of sentiment and not "hard data." The six-month outlook is also less reliable than the current data, he says.

Still, sentiment is much of what drives the business world. And if sentiment is weak, it's unlikely to augur a robust economy.

EXEC SUMMARY: PHILADELPHIA FED: BUSINESS OUTLOOK SURVEY

When to look: Noon ET on the third Thursday of the month.

Where to look: Go to *The Wall Street Journal* online's "Market Data Center" at www.WSJMarkets.com. When you are there, you'll need to go to the "Calendars & Economy" section and look under "U.S. Economic Events" for "Philadelphia Fed." Alternatively, for the full report go directly to the Philadelphia Federal Reserve, which publishes the Business Outlook Survey each month and makes it available at www.phil.frb.org/research-and-data/regional-economy/business-outlook-survey/.

What to watch for: Increases (decreases) in the diffusion index.

What it means: The economy is heating up (cooling down).

What steps to take: Buy (sell) riskier assets like stocks and high yield corporate debt and get out of (into) safer investments like government bonds and cash.

For the more adventurous, exploit information in one or more of the subindexes to pick out possible moves in specific industries or sectors.

Risk level: Medium to high.

Profit possibility: $$ to $$$

35

REAL INTEREST RATES
(Leading)

Fed watching, or trying to work out the policy stance of the Federal Reserve, has historically been a mind-numbing experience. Listening to testimony from its governors and various chiefs gives new meaning to the description of economics as a "dismal science."

It doesn't necessarily need to be that way. We can learn a lot about what the Fed is trying to do by looking at so-called real interest rates. That's actually both quite simple to do and quite revealing at the same time.

"It's a good measure of the accommodative nature of monetary policy," says Guy LeBas, chief fixed income strategist at investment banking firm Janney Montgomery Scott in Philadelphia.

To work out the real interest rate you adjust the stated, or nominal, interest rate for the withering effects of inflation.

(Real interest rate = nominal interest rate minus inflation.) Or, in other words, what goods and services will the money you invest in government securities buy you when you get back the principal plus interest?

If it won't buy you as much as it would now, then the real interest rate is said to be negative. If it will buy you more in the future, then the real interest rate is positive.

So what? Well, the simple fact of knowing whether real interest rates are positive or negative tells you a lot about the policy of the Federal Reserve. Specifically, it tells us whether the Fed has an accommodating policy or a restrictive policy.

Accommodative policy is when real interest rates are negative and is conducive to speeding up economic growth. Restrictive policy, when real rates are positive, tends to slow down growth in the economy.

The lower real interest rates are, the more borrowers want to borrow, bolstering the consumption and investment components of the economy. As real interest rates increase, people want to borrow less, and that hurts investment and consumption.

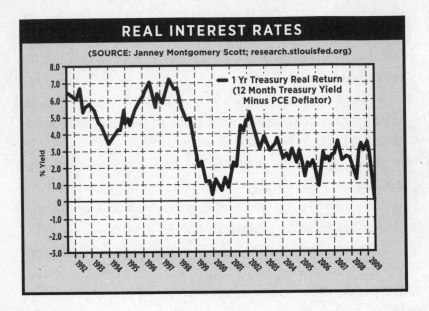

Investment Strategy

Real interest rates rise during expansions and fall during recessions, largely due to changes in demand for money. Real interest rates typically fall before a recovery as nominal interest rates stay flat and inflation expectations rise.

There have been a couple of times in history when a central bank lowering the cost of borrowing had little effect on stimulating the economy: for example, the United States during the Great Depression and Japan during its Great Stagnation (1990–present). The reason is simple: People expected deflation, or a fall in the general prices for goods and services. That meant "real interest rates" remained high, too high for an economic recovery.

Real interest rates have implications for investors also. "In theory, if real interest rates are negative, no matter what you throw your money into you should make a profit," says Janney's LeBas. "The theory breaks from reality in that short-term market volatility can always beat out a profit."

LeBas points to commodities in general and industrial metals in particular as assets that do well during times of negative real interest rates. He suggests avoiding the stocks of metals companies, as that exposes investors to stock market risk.

Conversely, he says, when real interest rates are high, that's a good time to look at the bond market. He also notes that it has been decades since real interest rates were high in the United States.

One other important tip: LeBas says there are many ways to calculate real interest rates with much of the problem centered on how to measure inflation. LeBas favors the Personal Consumption Expenditure (PCE) deflator used in the calculation of gross domestic product, as it takes into account the changing preferences of consumers.

"CPI [Consumer Price Index] assumes that someone who bought a basket of goods a year ago will buy the same basket of goods today," he says. "That's not necessarily the case: If Brie prices rise, they may go with Stilton instead."

EXEC SUMMARY: REAL INTEREST RATES

When to look: Daily, or as new data on either interest rates or inflation comes out.

Where to look: To calculate this indicator you'll need to look for two pieces of data. Take a nominal interest rate series and subtract a measure of inflation, be it CPI, PPI, the GDP PCE deflator, or some other measure. The data for inflation and nominal interest rates can be found at *The Wall Street Journal* online's "Market Data Center." You'll find the data center at www.WSJMarkets.com. Inflation data will be found within the "Calendars & Economy" section, whereas interest rate information will be within the "Bonds, Rates & Credit Markets" section.

Or find the necessary data at FRED, which also has data on TIPS or Treasury Inflation-Protected Securities. Under normal market conditions, TIPS can serve as a direct measure of inflation expectations. See http://research.stlouisfed.org/fred2/categories/82. However, under abnormal conditions, like during the Great Credit Crunch of 2008–9, the value of TIPS declined so much that the indication of inflation expectations was erroneous.

What to watch for: Increases (decreases) in real interest rates.

What it means: The economy will shrink (grow) in the near future.

What steps to take: Buy hard assets when real interest rates are negative, but beware short-term fluctuations. Buy bonds when real interest rates are positive as nominal interest rates will probably move lower, sparking a bull market for bonds.

Risk level: Medium to high.

Profit possibility: $$ to $$$

36

SHORT INTEREST
Leading

B ETTING AGAINST A COMPANY seems un-American. We are after all a nation of optimists. Still, we can learn something from the naysayers, notably those who bet against the stocks of publicly traded companies. These so-called short sellers make money when stocks go down in price and we can use their activity as an investment indicator.

Short sellers bet against a publicly traded company by selling stock that they have borrowed. The short seller profits if the price of the shares goes down before he has to return the borrowed stock. It's just sell high and buy low, instead of buy low and sell high.

The total amount of stock sold short of a particular company is known as short interest. To be absolutely precise, short interest is an investment indicator, not an economic one, but it is included here because the two are very closely related. Also, it's worth noting that this book is about indicators and how to use them to make money. In that regard, this one fits the bill.

Selling shares short attracts a massive amount of negative publicity. Perhaps not surprisingly, managers of publicly traded firms often dislike their companies' shares being shorted. Occasionally, the government temporarily bans shorting certain types of stock, such as with some banks/financial shares during the height of the financial crisis in 2008.

Despite the bad publicity, the information that short sellers give us is very useful. That's because short interest is a contrary indicator. In the simplest terms, when many shares of a stock have been sold short it's bullish for the stock price.

The number of shares sold short represents a "well" of potential buying power. The reason: Shorts can't stay short forever. Eventually short sellers must return the shares they borrowed and sold. There are a couple of financial reasons for this. When you sell shares short you must pay interest for borrowing them plus the value of the dividends due the lender. In addition, if the price of the stock goes up, then the broker that lent the shares may ask for collateral to cover any losses.

Such rallies sometimes force short sellers who can't post the extra collateral to buy back stock to "cover" the short position. That extra buying can send the stock even higher. In simple terms, high short interest can be a bullish sign for a stock.

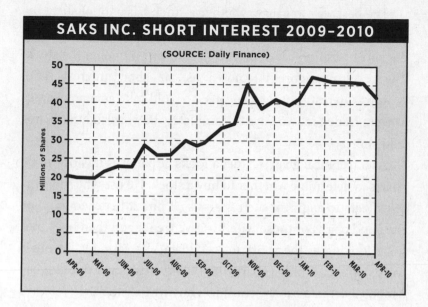

SAKS INC. SHORT INTEREST 2009–2010

(SOURCE: Daily Finance)

Investment Strategy

On average, stock prices have trended upward over long periods, so indiscriminately shorting shares is likely not a winning strategy. Successful short sellers must look for specific reasons for a specific share to decline, as they did with Lehman Brothers in 2008.

But quite frequently short sellers are wrong. And when they are, savvy investors can profit.

The trick is to find a stock not only with relatively high short interest, but that is also a well-run and attractively valued company, says Adolfo Rueda, a technical analyst at WJB Capital Group in New York. "That tells me someone has the fundamentals incorrect."

The best way to gauge whether a stock has a lot of short interest is to look at how many days it would take to cover the net short position based on recent trading volume in the stock. The resulting figure is known as the short interest ratio. A short interest ratio of 2 means it would take as many shares as were traded in two days to completely buy back all the shares sold short.

As a technical analyst, Rueda looks at patterns in stock price charts to determine whether to buy a stock. He uses the short interest data to augment such analysis. "I find it better to look for the good charts or those with positive trend, and then back into it by looking at the short interest data," he says. Or, in other words, when he finds a chart with bullish trends and one that has a lot of short interest, he considers buying the stock.

The same approach would work for someone who analyzes a company by reading financial statements. Rueda says it's probably not smart to draw too many conclusions from looking at short interest in exchange-traded funds like those that track major stock market indices, such as the SPDR S&P 500 (SPY) ETF.

The problem is that some money managers use such ETFs for sophisticated hedging activity that sometimes has little to do with whether they expect a specific index to decline or not.[3]

"It kinda skews the data," Rueda says.

---

[3] For instance, a fund manager who expects, say, a bank stock to outperform its peer group may sell short an ETF that holds a broad basket of bank stocks and then use the proceeds of the short sale to buy the stock that is expected to outperform. That way even if the entire group—including the favored stock—drops in price but the favored stock still does better, the money manager will have made a profit.

EXEC SUMMARY: SHORT INTEREST

When to look: Each business day.

Where to look: Some useful data on short interest is found in *The Wall Street Journal* online's "Market Data Center" at www.WSJ Markets.com. When you are there, you'll need to go to the "U.S. Stocks" tab and look for "Quarterly/Monthly Snapshots," where you will find a list of the biggest short positions.

In addition, major exchanges like the NYSE and NASDAQ publish short interest reports. DailyFinance.com also provides short interest data, including the short interest ratio, as does http://short squeeze.com/.

What to watch for: Increases in the short interest ratio of a company with good management and solid fundamentals or a bullish technical trend.

What it means: Short sellers may have bitten off more than they can chew.

What steps to take: Buy the company's shares and hope that the shorts will bid up the price when they "cover," or buy shares to return them to the lender.

Risk level: Astronomical.

Profit possibility: $$$$

37

RUSSELL 2000
Leading

(See also Risk Structure of Interest Rates)

I F YOU LIVE IN America, chances are you work for a small company. Small businesses fuel most job creation, but they are more risky than larger enterprises.

It's that extra risk and investor attitude toward it that can help us learn a lot about the broader economy. Try to envision a small boat on the ocean next to a large warship. Waves knock the smaller vessel hither and thither while the larger vessel remains stable. The same is true of companies getting knocked about by economic shocks.

Investors know investing in smaller companies is riskier than investing in larger ones. But they also know that smaller companies benefit much more from fairer economic conditions than big ones do, just as smaller boats benefit more from calmer seas than larger ships.

That's where the Russell 2000 comes in: It helps us measure investor risk appetite, and from that we can infer how the economy is doing. Specifically, the Russell 2000 (RUT) Index tracks two thousand smaller publicly traded stocks. The index itself is the one against which most mutual fund managers specializing in small capitalization (small cap) stocks are benchmarked.

What "capitalization" means is: "How much is this company worth?" It specifically refers to the dollar value of all of a company's outstanding stock at its current stock price. That's the easy bit.

What counts as "small" is a bit of a moving target that changes over time. For the most part, think about companies worth less than $1 billion. The average market cap of companies in the Russell 2000 was around $400 million in mid-2010, according to Russell Investments' website. Or put another way, the average firm in the index is a so-called small cap worth less than half a billion dollars—pretty small potatoes these days.

That compares with over $170 billion for General Electric on the same date, for instance. Clearly, the Russell 2000 stocks are tiny in comparison.

So what can we learn by looking at this index? "If the broader indices like the S&P 500 (GSPC) are meandering along and the small caps are up, then you might be seeing risk appetite return," says Barry Ritholtz, CEO of New York–based asset management firm Fusion IQ, and author of *Bailout Nation*.

The good news about an increase in investor appetite for risky assets is it can presage economic expansion. If the move is matched in the real economy, with businesses buying new machinery and equipment, then small companies will tend to do well.

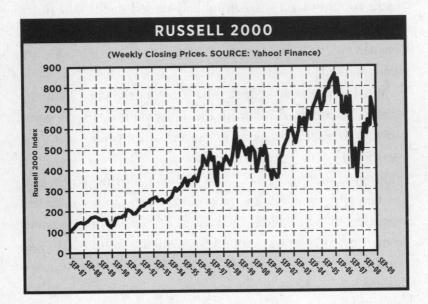

RUSSELL 2000

(Weekly Closing Prices. SOURCE: Yahoo! Finance)

Investment Strategy

The problem with any index is that markets can sometimes be volatile. Twentieth-century economist John Maynard Keynes put it well: "Markets can remain irrational longer than you can remain solvent."

For that reason Ritholtz says it's important not to jump to erroneous conclusions. For instance, he says when the Russell 2000 jumped in late 2009 and early 2010, the quick rise may have been due to greater risk appetite, but it also may have been because the index had been so badly pummeled earlier in the year.

Stocks are often observed to bounce back somewhat following a long period of falling. Some call this a "technical bounce," others a "dead cat bounce." Sometimes it has little to do with changes in the real economy or investor expectations.

Ritholtz says that market indices can be like an inkblot test where what is seen is open to a vast array of interpretations. For that reason he suggests guarding against "seeing" anything that isn't really there but that perhaps you'd like there to be. In other words, come to data with an open mind, not a preconceived notion that you are hell-bent on "proving" no matter what.

Good questions to ask yourself: Is there another reasonable explanation for the phenomenon I'm seeing? Do other pieces of data support the conclusion? This sort of skepticism works not only when looking at the Russell but also many of the other indicators in this book.

For those wanting to invest in the Russell 2000, probably the easiest way of doing so is through the iShares Russell 2000 Index Fund (IWM) exchange-traded fund, which tracks the value of the index.

EXEC SUMMARY: RUSSELL 2000

When to look: Continuously.

Where to look: For data on the Russell 2000, go to *The Wall Street Journal* online's "Market Data Center" at www.WSJMarkets

.com. When you are there, you'll need to go to the "U.S. Stocks" tab and look under "Other U.S. Indexes."

In addition, data on the Russell 2000 trading prices can be found at Yahoo! Finance at www.finance.yahoo.com. Details of the index itself can be found on Russell Investments' website at www.Russell.com.

What to watch for: Increases (decreases) in the Russell 2000.

What it means: The appetite for risk may be growing (shrinking) due to investor expectations about economic trends.

What steps to take: If you think the first upward (downward) movements in the index represent a change in sentiment rather than a technical dead cat bounce (minor correction), buy (sell) a Russell ETF.

Risk level: High.

Profit possibility: $$$

38

WEEKLY LEADING INDEX
Leading

(*See also* JoC-ECRI Industrial Price Index)

HERE'S A TALL ORDER: Develop a metric to give a relatively accurate read on the future state of the entire economy. Make it "see" not just one month down the road, but as far as eight months. And it needs to be timely too, so that there is time to take evasive action before the crash.

That's more or less what the Manhattan-based Economic Cycle Research Institute tried to do when it developed the Weekly Leading Index (WLI) in the 1980s. The people at ECRI basically spend all day every day figuring out the what and why of business cycles.

"[The WLI is] basically the sequel to the original leading indicator idea, which came into being in the 1960s," says Lakshman Achuthan, managing director at ECRI, referring to the Conference Board's much-admired leading economic indicator (LEI).

Achuthan says the inputs that make up the WLI include measures of the money supply, the JoC-ECRI Industrial Price Index, measures of housing activity, jobs and labor market indicators, equity prices, and some bond market prices.

In a couple of key ways, ECRI tried to improve on the original LEI, just like automobile engineers improved upon Henry Ford's classic Model T: First, the WLI's data comes out weekly, not monthly—so it's more timely. In addition, all but one of the numbers that make up the WLI never get revised.

"Revisions make a handy excuse for forecasters," says Achuthan. "So, we removed that excuse from ourselves."

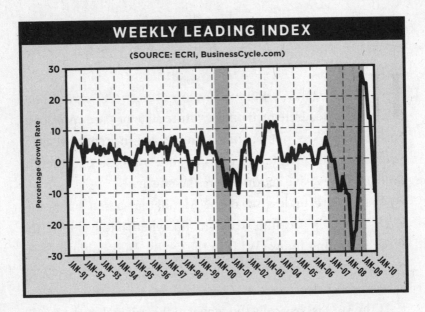

Investment Strategy

The big problem with many economists' forecasts is that they tell you, "On the one hand this, on the other hand that," says Achuthan.

This ambivalence makes it difficult to know what economists are really saying, if they are saying anything useful at all. Therefore, the WLI was designed as a one-armed economist. As he explains, "It gives you a directional call on the economic cycle without saying on the one hand this, but on the other . . ."

The trick is not in reading the WLI, but rather in interpreting it. Some people manage to misread the WLI and then get it wrong when they call the end or beginning of a recession. Achuthan says these misinterpretations often happen because what's needed, and not always used, is a disciplined approach to the metric.

ECRI claims never to have made a bad call on a recession ending or beginning. As with its other indicators, like the JoC-ECRI Industrial Price Index covered earlier in this book, ECRI uses the so-called three-P's approach whereby movements in the index that catch their attention are pronounced (big movement), persistent (lasts like the Energizer Bunny), *and* pervasive (based on numerous inputs, not just a few).

It's the last element that trips up many forecasters. For instance, following the spectacular drop in the stock market in 1987 the WLI dropped, but the move wasn't pervasive, because stocks were really the only element of the WLI to move. So

ECRI coolly and correctly shied off calling a recession despite the widespread fear in the markets.

Other forecasters weren't so levelheaded. If, on the other hand, there is a turn in the WLI growth rate that satisfies the three P's, then a recession (or the end of one) can be expected seven to eight months later.

"The WLI is very unemotional [and] it doesn't get caught up in the narrative of the day," Achuthan says.

It's important to note that the WLI is a measure of what's going to happen for the entire economy whereas the JoC-ECRI Industrial Price Index specifically focuses in on the industrial sector and perhaps for that reason is better suited to gauging the health of manufacturing.

EXEC SUMMARY: WEEKLY LEADING INDEX

When to look: Weekly at 10:30 a.m. ET.

Where to look: The ECRI WLI data is posted free on www.businesscycle.com. It also probably pays to scour the press for nuggets in order to get ECRI's calls on whether the economy is going to boom or flop.

What to watch for: Increases (decreases) in the WLI that are pronounced, persistent, and pervasive.

What it means: The economy is heating up (cooling down).

What steps to take: If Yoda were here, he would say something like: "When the WLI goes down, risky assets you should sell. Let The Force guide you to the safety of bonds and defensive stocks. When the WLI rises, as must it eventually, risky assets you should buy. Luke Skywalker have you seen recently?"

Risk level: Medium.

Profit possibility: $$

39

YIELD CURVE
Leading

Even for economists, monitoring the U.S. government securities market can be like watching paint dry. Still, for those with the patience to do so, it can yield big profits.

But first you need to know what to look for and what it means. What to watch is the difference between the yields on long-term government securities (ten-year bonds, a.k.a. ten-year T-note) and the yields on short-term ones (the three-month Treasury bill).

Monitoring the difference in rates is known as watching the yield curve, and it can help identify turning points in the economy, such as the beginning of a recession. (A plot of the yields of more than two maturities of government securities produces a curve on a chart.)

When the difference in yields is negative—in other words,

when the yield on the ten-year Treasury note is lower than the yield on the three-month T-bill—the chance of a recession four quarters later rises dramatically. Even more interestingly, the higher the T-bill rate is above the ten-year T-note rate the greater is the likelihood of a recession.

"It is one of the better indicators out there," says Anthony Crescenzi, strategist and portfolio manager at Newport Beach, California–based bond-fund giant Pimco. He points to a classic 1995 National Bureau of Economic Research (NBER) study by Arturo Estrella and Frederic Mishkin that detailed how the difference between the ten-year note and the three-month bill was highly correlated with economic activity one year in the future.

Why is this indicator so powerful? One simple way to think about it is that the long-term interest rate (the ten-year T-note) is a cumulative bet on where the short-term rate will be, explains Crescenzi. In other words, the ten-year rate is the one-year rate ten times.

A falling ten-year rate then suggests that short-term rates will be heading south. Why? Likely because the Federal Reserve, the U.S. Central Bank, will lower rates in response to weak economic conditions.

"One could say about the yield curve that it's the combined judgment of millions of investors around the world," says Crescenzi. "The expectations of investors are embedded in those yields across the curve."

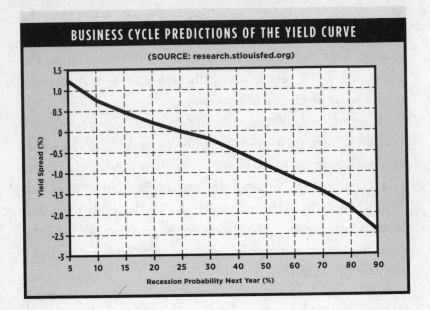

Investment Strategy

Mishkin and Estrella's paper lays out a relationship that we've replicated here showing the increasing probability of a U.S. recession the more negative the difference between the ten-year T-note and the three-month T-bill is.

Notably, when the yield curve is simply flat—the difference in rates is approximately zero—the chance of a recession one year later is 25%, or one in four. The chances of a slump rise to approximately 70% when the spread widens to minus 1.5 percentage points.

Best of all, because it's so forward looking, investors have plenty of time to act on the information. Specifically, if you spy a recession on the horizon, then one strategy is to start looking to move away from so-called risky assets toward less risky ones, says Crescenzi.

In this case, investors should stay away from junk-rated debt investments (so-called high yield) in favor of high-quality bonds or government securities that will rise in value as interest rates fall.

Look also to avoid shares of companies that are seen as economically sensitive, like home builders and retailers. Instead, Crescenzi suggests, buy defensive stocks like those that sell consumer staples or cater to budget-conscious consumers.

EXEC SUMMARY: YIELD CURVE

When to look: Continuously.

Where to look: *The Wall Street Journal* publishes the yield curve daily, in classic chart format. Data on yields of different maturities of Treasury securities can be found in *The Wall Street Journal* online's "Market Data Center" at www.WSJMarkets.com. When you are there, you'll need to go to the "Bonds, Rates & Credit Markets" tab.

Alternatively, you can find the data in the FRED database at the St. Louis Fed.

The Mishkin paper is available all over the Web. Here's one place to grab it: http://ideas.repec.org/p/nbr/nberwo/5279.html.[4]

---

[4] While Mishkin and Estrella get much of the credit for modern yield curve theory, Duke's Cam Harvey presaged their efforts. If you want to delve deeper into the predictive powers of yield curves and don't mind a little mathematics, check out Cam's 1986 University of Chicago dissertation "Recovering Expectations of Consumption Growth from an Equilibrium Model of the Term Structure of Interest Rates," his 1988 *Journal of Financial Economics* article, "The Real Term Structure and Consumption Growth," or other work available at www.duke.edu/~charvey/research_term_structure.htm.

What to watch for: Increases (decreases) in the spread between long- and short-term Treasuries.

What it means: The economy is heating up (cooling down). The higher the short-term interest rate rises over the long-term one, the more likely the economy is headed into recession.

What steps to take: Appropriate cyclical investments, e.g., buy high-quality bonds and consumer staples and avoid high-risk securities when it looks like the economy is cooling down.

Risk level: Medium.

Profit possibility: $$

INFLATION, FEAR, AND UNCERTAINTY

OUR REMAINING ELEVEN INDICATORS are arguably the most important of all because they point to the possible approach of the three horsemen of the apocalypse. Well, the investment apocalypse anyway. They are inflation, fear, and uncertainty.

Often, they are absolutely crucial to seeing impending recessions before the investing herd does because they can presage major downticks in the GDP components of consumption, investment, government, imports, exports, and the combination indicators (C, I, G, and NX). When inflation, fear, or uncertainty rear their ugly heads, a rapid response can save investors a bundle and greatly reward the bold and the brave.

40

GDP DEFLATOR

Coincident

(*See also* Producer Price Index, Big Mac Index)

INFLATION MATTERS BECAUSE IT'S like a silent tax. In good times it slowly eats away at the purchasing power of your money or cash. In bad times it has a voracious appetite and quickly renders paper money worthless.

This silent tax hurts those who can least afford it: the poor and those on fixed incomes. Undoubtedly it contributed to strife between the world wars in Germany when people needed wheelbarrows full of cash to buy basic foods. Because of these consequences, economists, politicians, and the public take note of it.

There are many measures of inflation, and not one of them is perfect. But the GDP deflator has significant merits, according to Michael Woolfolk, managing director and foreign exchange strategist at Bank of New York Mellon.

The GDP deflator tells us how much the prices of goods and services rose during a given measurement period. It's used to "deflate the GDP" figures and tell us how much the economy grew in "real" terms. For that reason we see it come out once per quarter along with details of how much the economy grew.

The GDP deflator has an advantage over the more widely recognized CPI (Consumer Price Index). It tells us what prices did for all goods and services across the economy, whereas the CPI looks only at a relatively small basket of goods. That generally fixed basket can lead to distortions in measurement of inflation.

Woolfolk also points to the fact that U.S. CPI (Consumer Price Index, which tracks the changing price of a basket of goods and services) isn't really comparable across national boundaries.

"The GDP deflator is the most broad-based measure of inflation and arguably it is the most comparable to inflation measures in other countries," he says, noting that CPI calculations in different countries tend to use totally different metrics.

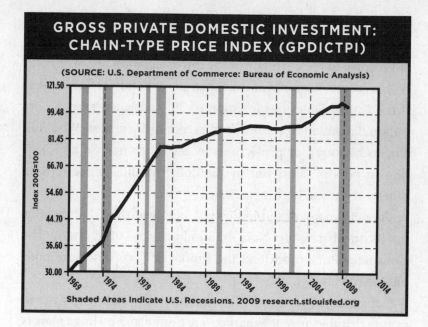

GROSS PRIVATE DOMESTIC INVESTMENT: CHAIN-TYPE PRICE INDEX (GPDICTPI)

(SOURCE: U.S. Department of Commerce: Bureau of Economic Analysis)

Shaded Areas Indicate U.S. Recessions. 2009 research.stlouisfed.org

Investment Strategy

Woolfolk uses the GDP deflator to help analyze the currency markets. That's generally considered to be a pretty tall order as currency markets are generally considered to be rather opaque. On top of that, governments have been known to intervene in currency markets, throwing off otherwise sound economic analysis.

However, Woolfolk gets a handle on one part of the problem—that of the economic analysis—by trying to adjust his forecasts for differences in *relative* inflation levels. The difference between the rates of inflation tells us how much faster the spending power of one currency is depreciating relative to the other. If all else stays the same, then that means the country with the higher inflation should see the value of its currency fall relative to the currency of the lower-inflation country.

He uses an example of the Japanese yen and the U.S. dollar. If the United States has inflation of 3% and Japan zero, a not-unfamiliar situation for much of recent history, then Woolfolk adjusts his currency projections by the difference. So a projection of one hundred yen to the dollar would be reduced to ninety-seven yen in this example.

As with many of the indicators, however, the GDP deflator has its drawbacks, too. Notably, it only comes out quarterly. The Consumer Price Index and the Producer Price Index are both published monthly.

Separately, if using this data for currency trading, it's worth noting that the currency markets are dominated by huge players including central banks (like the Bank of England) and massive commercial banks like Citigroup. That means small investors often stand to lose when investing in them. Be cautious before dipping a toe into the currency markets!

EXEC SUMMARY: GDP DEFLATOR

When to look: At 8:30 a.m. ET, the third or fourth week of the month. The data comes out in tandem with GDP. There are three estimates given to each quarter's data.

Where to look: To get the GDP deflator data, go to *The Wall Street Journal* online's "Market Data Center" at www.WSJMarkets.com.

When you are there, you'll need to go to the "Calendars & Economy" section and look under "U.S. Economic Events" for "GDP." The GDP deflator is the same thing as the GDP price index.

Alternatively, the FRED database publishes the GDP deflator, as does the Bureau of Economic Analysis at www.bea.gov. It's also easy to get data from the free "Investor" section of the website Briefing.com.

What to watch for: Changes in relative inflation rates between two countries.

What it means: The currency of the country experiencing more inflation will eventually depreciate vis-à-vis the other.

What steps to take: Buy the currency experiencing relatively less inflation and sit out the short-term fluctuations and government interventions that regularly rock foreign exchange markets.

Risk level: Astronomical.

Profit possibility: $$$$

41

GOLD PRICE
Leading

YOU'VE HEARD OF THE golden rule—whoever has the gold makes the rules. It's trite—rather like saying, be richer.

What isn't so trivial is the fact that gold can be used as a measuring stick of sentiment. Broadly speaking, gold is a highly sensitive barometer of all things dodgy economically, financially, and geopolitically.

When the economy is robust, the financial system is sound, and the world is not involved in major upheaval, investors don't tend to buy gold, and prices for the metal tend to remain subdued.

During the 1980s and 1990s, for example, most investors shunned gold, preferring other investments. As a result, gold remained in a bear market for the two decades from 1980 through 1999, during which the price fell from a peak of $850 to a low around $250 an ounce. That also coincided with great times economically: high growth, low inflation, and no prolonged wars.

Contrast that with the decade starting 2001. During that time gold prices have more than quintupled from around $260 an ounce to over $1,300 by late 2010. That coincided with the bursting of the tech bubble, the rise and fall of a speculative mania in U.S. real estate, the near crippling of the world banking system, and the drawn-out involvement by the United States in two major wars: Iraq and Afghanistan. On top of that the U.S. government is borrowing unsustainable amounts of money, raising the threat of inflation.

That's where gold steps in as a viable investment. The metal has been shown to be a store of value over the very long term, while paper money invariably loses much of its value within mere decades if not more quickly. Veteran gold investor George Gero points out that in the 1930s a kilo of gold would buy you a nice four-door car; it will still do exactly the same thing today. That's despite the fact that a dollar, or any other currency, will buy you a tiny fraction of what it once did.

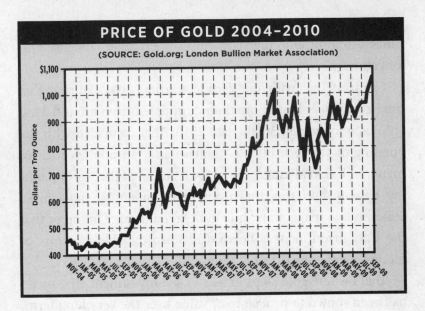

PRICE OF GOLD 2004–2010

(SOURCE: Gold.org; London Bullion Market Association)

Investment Strategy

The key to using gold as a sentiment indicator is watching investment demand for the metal. About two-thirds of the gold produced in the world goes into making jewelry. But what is most correlated with surges in the gold price is how much gold *investors* are socking away.

Jeff Christian, head of New York–based commodities consulting firm CPM Group, notes that the gold price tends to do well when investment demand is over 20 million ounces a year.

"We are still using that rubric," says Christian. The big difference now is that investors are snapping up even greater quantities and look set to continue doing so, he says.

So how do you use this information to make some money? You could try to follow the smart money and invest in gold when investors are buying lots of the metal. However, that might be better left to professionals like Christian because the gold market is murky to say the least.

What you can do, though, is use gold as portfolio insurance, or insurance against economic catastrophes. "My view has always been that a portion of your portfolio should be designed to protect against disasters," says Christian, who has been actively watching the gold market since the mid-1970s. "But most of your portfolio should be designed to benefit from more probable economic scenarios."

Or put another way, put a percentage of your portfolio into gold. The price of gold has been shown to be uncorrelated with the prices of other assets, and that lack of correlation means that it reduces the swings in the overall value of an investment portfolio. If the worst happens, then the value of the gold will likely appreciate. If the worst doesn't happen, then the other investments will do well. Most professionals think putting 5–15% of your total portfolio into gold is appropriate.

There are a few methods of buying gold. The simplest is the SPDR Gold Shares exchange-traded fund (GLD), which is bought just like stocks. You can also buy physical gold in the form of coins. But make certain to purchase only bullion coins, those whose value is determined by the gold content and not by finish or rarity. Popular coins include American Eagles, South African Krugerrands, and Canadian Maple Leafs.

EXEC SUMMARY: GOLD PRICE

When to look: Gold is traded most business days.

Where to look: For gold prices, go to *The Wall Street Journal* online's "Market Data Center" at www.WSJMarkets.com. When you are there, you'll need to go to the "Commodities & Futures" section and look for gold under the metals section.

In addition, World Gold Council has a wealth of information on all things gold at Gold.org. It sponsors the largest gold exchange-traded fund, the SPDR Gold Shares, and provides daily information on how much gold is held by the fund.

The World Gold Council works closely with London-based consulting firm GFMS Ltd. to publish research. CPM also publishes books on gold, which contain hard-to-obtain historical data as well as market commentary.

The London Bullion Market Association, LBMA.org.uk, dominates the trade in gold and publishes a reference price known as the "fix." The price isn't rigged. The fix is much like the settlement price on U.S. futures exchanges.

Also check out Kitco.com, the website of the Montreal-based gold dealer.

What to watch for: Changes in prices and quantities indicating that supply and/or demand for gold is shifting.

What it means: When demand for gold increases, investors fear inflation, even economic implosion, or geopolitical instability.

What steps to take: Buy (short) gold on the first hint of inflation or catastrophe, man-made or natural (signs of long-term price level and financial system stability).

Risk level: High.

Profit possibility: $$$

42

MISERY INDEX
Coincident to Leading

WHEN THE ECONOMICS GODS are smiling, we see our paychecks get fatter and the goods we buy get cheaper. Don't laugh. It's been known to happen. But sometimes we get the opposite. We see our paychecks disappear (lose our jobs) and the costs of everything we need to buy skyrockets (inflation). That's economic misery.

We can't be sure because he's not alive to ask, but economic and social misery were likely at the forefront of economist Arthur Okun's mind when he developed the Misery Index (MI). Like so many brilliant ideas, the MI is simple. It just adds the unemployment rate together with the inflation rate. The higher the figure, the more misery society has to deal with.

"The Misery Index captures the pain throughout the economy," says Peter Rodriguez, professor of economics at the Darden Business School, University of Virginia. "It's most acute among the lowest rungs on the economic ladder."

It makes sense that the MI was developed in the 1970s, when for the first time since the 1860s the government's (or the gold standard's) tight hold on inflation came unstuck, explains Rodriguez. During that same dreadful decade came levels of unemployment not seen since the Great Depression of the 1930s. Under the economic theories prevailing in the seventies, high inflation and high unemployment were incompatible; the former would automatically create jobs and the latter would naturally keep prices down. However, the theories were wrong.

"This phenomenon of high unemployment and rising inflation was a new thing altogether and we had the 'dismal science' turning into the 'miserable science,'" says Rodriguez. A similar index invented by economist Robert Barro, the Barro Misery Index, also uses inflation and unemployment but adds in other variables too.

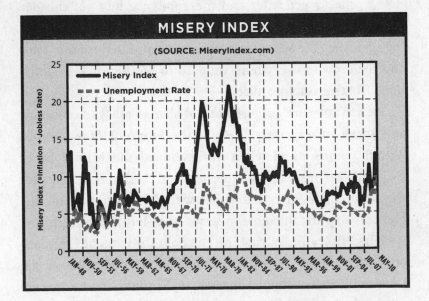

Investment Strategy

"For the most part this is a very blue-collar index," says Rodriguez. However, that is not to say that those higher up the ladder don't feel something also, he adds.

Because of the way economic pain is felt, we can use the Misery Index as a crude metric to help read the electoral tea leaves. Or more simply put, when the Misery Index is high and rising, then you can expect the general populace to be hopping mad.

And sometimes they hop madly to the polling place, where they take out their frustrations on incumbents, as when they ousted Democratic president Jimmy Carter. When Carter took office, the Misery Index was a fairly elevated 12.7, but close to the low of his one-term presidency. It jumped to the record high (of any presidency) of about 22 in June 1980. Needless to say, Carter lost to Ronald Reagan in a Republican landslide.

Those presidents who somehow managed to see the Misery Index drop or stay relatively flat tended to make it through two terms—George W. Bush and Bill Clinton are two examples.

"Either the president must improve the overall economic conditions or he won't get a second chance," says Rodriguez.

The Misery Index also tells us how well the Federal Reserve is doing. Rodriguez points out the Fed, unlike other central banks, has a double mandate of low inflation and low unemployment. So the higher the Misery Index, the worse the job the Fed is doing.

What investors can do with the MI is a tricky, contextual question. They might use the MI to predict "gridlock" in Washington, which might be bullish for stocks. Or they might use it to help read the interest rate tea leaves. The Fed is pretty independent from the political process, but it is not completely immune as it enjoys no constitutional protection.

EXEC SUMMARY: MISERY INDEX

When to look: Whenever inflation or unemployment rates change.

Where to look: You can get the components of the Misery Index—the unemployment rate and the CPI inflation rate—yourself by going to *The Wall Street Journal* online's "Market Data Center" www.WSJMarkets.com.

The same data is also available at the Bureau of Labor Statistics website, www.bls.gov.

Alternatively, you can get your data already downloaded along with details of who was in the White House at that time at www .MiseryIndex.us/.

What to watch for: A rising (falling) Misery Index.

What it means: Incumbent politicians are in deep doo-doo (have it made in the shade) and Fed bashing will be on the rise (decline).

What steps to take: Look for changes (the status quo) in Washington and at the Fed.

Risk level: That depends on what you do with the MI. If you bet a million bucks even money on the next presidential election we'd consider that pretty risky. If you use the index in conjunction with the other forty-nine discussed in this book to place small bets, then we'd say that it is pretty low.

Profit possibility: $ to $$$$

43

PRODUCER PRICE INDEX

Leading into Recessions,
Coincident into Expansions

(*See also* GDP Deflator, Gold Prices, TIPS Spreads)

INFLATION ISN'T BORN IN the supermarket. Rather stores inherit it as the prices of goods they buy from their suppliers rise. That's why looking at the prices of the things that producers sell gives us a special window into where consumer prices might be going. For that we go to the aptly named Producer Price Index or PPI.

The PPI is a measure of inflation that is much less famous than its cousin, the CPI or Consumer Price Index. Instead of measuring how much a basket of goods and services costs individual consumers as the CPI does, the PPI measures how much domestic producers receive for their outputs or, looked at from the other side, how much retailers pay for the goods they sell.

"PPI tells us about business costs," says Peter Rodriguez, professor of economics at the Darden Business School, University of Virginia. "When the economy adjusts, some of the first indications of that change will be seen in producers' prices."

In recessionary times producers are under stress to survive, so they will lower their costs and cut prices or wages. Also, in order to keep their customers happy they will often try to cushion price increases from the final consumers.

But when times are good, prices get passed on to consumers immediately.

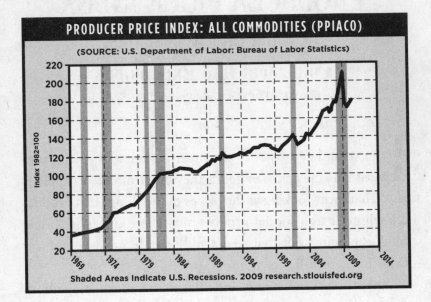

PRODUCER PRICE INDEX: ALL COMMODITIES (PPIACO)

(SOURCE: U.S. Department of Labor: Bureau of Labor Statistics)

Shaded Areas Indicate U.S. Recessions. 2009 research.stlouisfed.org

Investment Strategy

The PPI includes a number of different components including two very volatile elements: food and energy. That instability makes looking at the overall figure rather tricky for economists and investors. So to make things easier they strip out the food and energy prices and look at the so-called core rate. The idea here is that it's easier to spot trends when there is less volatility in the index.

And trends are the real key with the PPI. Rodriguez says, "Look for multimonth trends." More specifically he says it's worth looking at the "highest frequency moving averages," like an average of the last three or five months. When you plot those averages, then you can look for trends within those averages.

Specifically try this: Over time take an average of the prior three months annualized PPI rate and plot it on a chart. These so-called rolling averages iron out the volatility in the month-to-month data. If you can see a clear trend, then you can start to draw conclusions.

For instance, if the average inflation for the prior three months rises from 1% to 2%, then 3% over the period of June, July, and August, then there is clearly a trend of rising inflation. Whereas if the three-month moving average was 4% in one month followed by a decline of 2% and then a rise of 1%, it would be hard to argue that inflation is becoming a problem.

An upward trend could mean inflation at the retail level coming down the road. Or if the economy is weak it could mean the profit margins of retailers and producers alike will be squeezed.

Falling prices are trickier to analyze. They might fall due to a weak economy or it might be because of efficiency gains at the manufacturing level, says Rodriguez.

Rodriguez says Treasury Inflation-Protected Securities (TIPS) are a good way to beat inflation relative to regular bonds. Regular bonds pay interest and principal only on the "nominal" face value of the security rather than the spending power of the original bond.

If TIPS don't appeal, he says you might choose to hold your

assets in a less inflationary currency. He also points to gold as a useful, albeit volatile, hedge.

EXEC SUMMARY: PRODUCER PRICE INDEX

When to look: At 8:30 a.m. ET around the middle of the month.

Where to look: Editors and writers at *The Wall Street Journal* watch the PPI closely. As news about it is released, *Journal* reporters file breaking news stories for publication on WSJ.com.

If it's just the data you are looking for, go to *The Wall Street Journal* online's "Market Data Center" at www.WSJMarkets.com. You'll need to look under the "Calendars & Economy" tab for "U.S. Economic Events" and find "Producer Price Index."

Alternatively, you could go to the source: the Bureau of Labor Statistics, which computes the PPI. See www.bls.gov/pPI/. Historical data is available on the FRED database at http://research.stlouisfed.org/fred2/series/PPIACO?cid=31.

Briefing.com also has the information readily available in its free "Investor" section on its website.

What to watch for: Unexpected increases (decreases) in the core PPI three- or five-month moving average.

What it means: Inflation may be about to go wild (remain tame).

What steps to take: Get into (out of) inflation hedges like TIPS, gold, or less inflationary currencies.

Risk level: High.

Profit possibility: $$$

44

RETAIL INVESTMENT ACTIVITY
Leading into Recessions, Lagging during Recoveries

S OME PEOPLE ARE JUST born unlucky—so unlucky in fact that they do just the opposite of what they should at exactly the wrong time. Suckers? Maybe. But in the business of investing, those people have a name: retail investors.

Economists and investors can learn a lot by watching a group that has historically made very poor decisions when putting their own money to work. Specifically, we're talking about the "little guy." When the little guys invest in any asset class in a big way, be it stocks or houses, the easy profits are usually almost over.

"I tend to think that retail investors will hear about things when it's too late," says Peter Welgoss, research analyst at Financial Research Corporation (FRC) in Boston, Massachusetts. "It's one of those things that has plagued small investors for a long time."

FRC collects and collates data on investments in mutual funds, a product favored by most small investors. We can get a handle on what the retail investor is doing by using that data and then in certain cases doing the exact opposite.

Why? Because the little guys tend to do the opposite of what the savvy institutional investor does. Small investors tend to buy at or near the high points for the market, usually when the "smart" money is bailing. Likewise retail investors tend to sell when market prices are at or near their lows, when perhaps they should be buying.

"That might just be a human nature panic button effect," explains Welgoss.

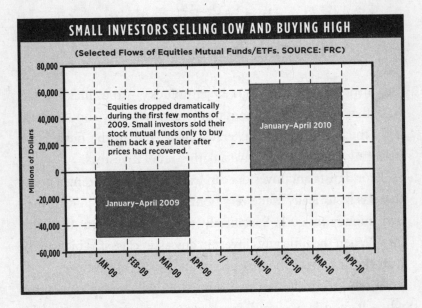

SMALL INVESTORS SELLING LOW AND BUYING HIGH

(Selected Flows of Equities Mutual Funds/ETFs. SOURCE: FRC)

Equities dropped dramatically during the first few months of 2009. Small investors sold their stock mutual funds only to buy them back a year later after prices had recovered.

January–April 2010

January–April 2009

Investment Strategy

FRC tracks how much money investors plow into mutual funds each month by using sophisticated techniques to estimate how much money either flowed into or out of a particular fund.

FRC's mutual fund data is important because it isolates what retail investors are doing. Professional investors tend not to invest in mutual funds. Instead they might use exchange-traded funds for stock market investments, or buy individual bonds in the fixed income market. Rich individuals also tend not to buy mutual funds. Instead they employ money managers to tailor a portfolio specifically for their needs.

Of course there are exceptions to these rules. But in general they hold true enough for us to use the flows of money into and out of mutual funds as a proxy for retail investor sentiment.

Because the mutual funds are typically categorized by the type of asset they invest in—stocks, bonds, cash, precious metals, domestic or international—we can see which categories of funds saw the biggest inflow and which saw the biggest outflow. That means you can see which asset types small investors went crazy for and which they fled.

If we combine that with information about the performance of certain assets, we can get an idea of whether an asset type is either entering a bubble or whether it is unfairly being dumped.

For instance, if returns on bond funds have been healthy and you see retail investors piling in at historically high levels, then it might be worth evaluating whether it makes sense to follow the herd or to go in a different direction.

Sometimes the flow of money into a particular fund is the result of an advertising campaign that has little to do with consumer sentiment for a particular asset. So, as always, you need to do careful research.

EXEC SUMMARY: RETAIL INVESTMENT ACTIVITY

When to look: Catch as catch can.

Where to look: FRC doesn't provide the funds flow data to just anyone. You have to be a big corporation. However, their press releases about the monthly funds flow data tend to get written up in the business media and so details of the funds flows are available on the Web for those willing to dig a little bit.

In addition, data on most mutual funds is provided by Morningstar, and it should be possible to estimate (roughly) what the flows are by looking at the assets under management and seeing the difference in value between measurement periods. (You'll need to make slight adjustments to account for the underlying performance of the fund.)

What to watch for: Changes in retail investor sentiment as measured by investment flows into (out of) different types of mutual funds. More specifically, look for record flows of funds into (or out of) different asset classes.

What it means: A record outflow (inflow) of funds from a certain asset could signal that the end of a bear (bull) market is near.

What steps to take: Buy when the "little guy" sells and sell when he buys, especially when that is the opposite of what professional investors are doing.

Risk level: Medium.

Profit possibility: $$

45

CREDIT SPREADS: THE RISK STRUCTURE OF INTEREST RATES
Leading

(See also Ted Spread)

T AKING RISKS IS AT the heart of American-style capitalism. That doesn't mean you should take insane, swashbuckling risks like those taken by nutty thrill seekers or berserk warriors. Rather, it is taking risks for a profit that is the true essence of good business. Nowhere is this more quantifiable than in the bond market where big publicly traded companies go to borrow money by selling IOUs.

In simple terms, riskier companies pay more to borrow money than less risky ones. It makes sense. You wouldn't lend to a riskier company if you'd make the same money lending to a safer one. You'd want more return for the increased risk.

This difference in the cost of borrowing is called the credit spread. It is measured in many ways, but here we focus on the difference between the interest rates paid on the absolute highest grade of traded debt (that rated AAA) and that of a grade slightly better than junk bonds (rated BBB). (Ostensibly, specialized rating agencies rate debt based on the creditworthiness of the borrower.)

The size of this credit spread also changes over time, narrowing ahead of an economic recovery and then widening before an economic slowdown. The economics behind this changing relationship is quite simple, and they're also behind the predictive qualities of this indicator.

"Capital being put to work makes the world go round, economically speaking," says David Ranson, head of research at the Beverly Farms, Massachusetts–based economics consulting firm H. C. Wainwright & Co. Economics Inc. As the credit spreads widen, it means investors are pricing in a higher level of risk. That increased perception of risk tends to slow the flow of capital through the economy. Without enough capital, economic growth is choked off.

"This is what happened in October 2008," when spreads widened and capital stopped flowing, says Ranson. "Hence, you got a recession."

The good news is that the same thing happens in reverse. When credit spreads narrow, it's an indication that capital is flowing more freely through the economy. By doing so it fuels economic growth.

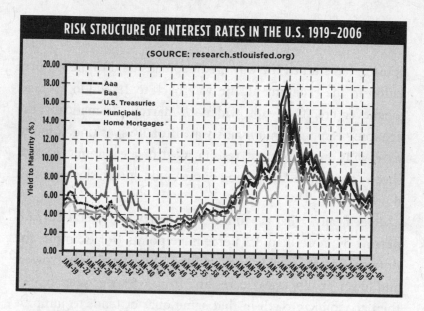

RISK STRUCTURE OF INTEREST RATES IN THE U.S. 1919–2006

(SOURCE: research.stlouisfed.org)

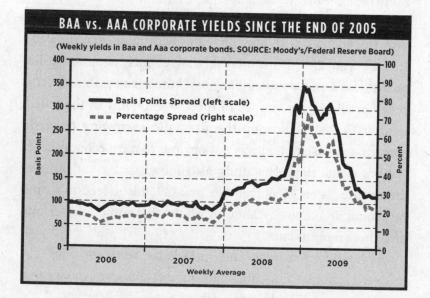

BAA vs. AAA CORPORATE YIELDS SINCE THE END OF 2005

(Weekly yields in Baa and Aaa corporate bonds. SOURCE: Moody's/Federal Reserve Board)

Investment Strategy

Ranson has studied the way credit spreads tend to move in relation to the economy all the way back to 1949. On average, whenever credit spreads widen or narrow dramatically the economy responds in a major way. Broadly speaking, a major narrowing in the spread results in strong economic growth shortly thereafter. A widening of the credit spread slows growth down.

Specifically, what he found was that when credit spreads narrow by more than 3.5 percentage points (for example, the difference in borrowing costs between high-quality borrowers and lower-quality ones decreasing from 6.5% per year to 3%), then economic growth in that same quarter tends to jump by more than 5% on average.

But more important, three to six months later economic growth explodes, with annualized growth rates exceeding 6%. In case you are in any doubt, that counts as smoking-hot growth for a rich country like the United States. Ranson correctly predicted the bounce in the U.S. economy in the fourth quarter of 2009 following the dramatic narrowing of credit spreads—an insight that was not obvious to most economic observers at the time. His study also found that a widening of credit spreads by 3.5 percentage points tends to lead to a drop in economic output by about 1.4% in that same quarter and also three months later.

So how do you make this knowledge work for you? The answer is simple: You choose to buy certain asset classes that will likely do well in the approaching economic scenario.

As credit spreads widen dramatically, it's safe to assume that an economic slowdown will follow relatively shortly thereafter. "At the onset of recession, seek out the investments that offer safety rather than risk in any form, or cyclicality," says Ranson.

Specifically, he says favor sovereign or government debt such as U.S. Treasury bonds—as well as gold as a safe-haven asset—and avoid commodities and equities of any type. (Ranson excludes gold from his definition of commodities. Instead he, like some others, sees it as its own special asset class.)

U.S. Treasuries can be purchased directly from the U.S. government at TreasuryDirect.gov. Small investors can get exposure to the price of gold bullion by considering the SPDR Gold Shares exchange-traded fund (GLD), which holds bars of gold. As credit spreads narrow, it signals that the economy is coming out of a recession. So the opposite investment advice applies. Investors should "embrace risk," says Ranson.

Also, emerging markets stocks can be good too as they tend to behave like hybrids combining commodities exposure and equity risks. Many emerging markets companies are engaged in commodity businesses like mining and agriculture.

EXEC SUMMARY: CREDIT SPREADS—THE RISK STRUCTURE OF INTEREST RATES

When to look: Each business day.

Where to look: *The Wall Street Journal* online's "Market Data Center" has some information on corporate debt yields. You'll find the data center at www.WSJMarkets.com. When you are there, you'll need to go to the "Bonds, Rates & Credit Markets" tab and look for the "Most Actives" in corporate bonds.

Other interest rate data for corporate bonds is widely available on the Internet. For easily searched and downloaded historical data, often going back decades, our favorite site is the FRED database at http://research.stlouisfed.org/fred2/. Also, private consulting firms like H. C. Wainwright & Co. Economics compile such data.

What to watch for: Narrowing (widening) credit spreads.

What it means: The economy is going to grow (shrink) that quarter and the next.

What steps to take: Buy stocks and commodities (buy short-term bonds and gold, or keep holdings in cash).

Risk level: Medium.

Profit possibility: $$

46

TED SPREAD
Leading

(*See also* Libor, Credit Availability Oscillator)

Following the great credit Crunch of 2008, it became really, really fashionable to hate banks. However, there is probably a more profitable way to express your anger. That's to figure out how banks feel about making loans and then making a killing.

Despite all the brouhaha and the hating, lending by banks is key to economic growth. It's actually quite easy to tell how bankers collectively feel about lending by looking at how they price the risk that loans won't be paid back.

Specifically, the question is how much more do the banks pay to lend to each other than the government pays to borrow? The U.S. government is considered to have zero risk that it won't pay its loans back. (It can tax and print money at will, after all.) So any interest rate charged over the government's rate is a measure of credit risk.

We can easily answer the question of how much more banks need to pay than does the government by calculating the Ted Spread, the difference between the yield on T-bills and Libor, the rate at which banks lend to each other.

"It represents the oxygen level in the financial markets," says David Rosenberg, chief economist and strategist at Toronto-based wealth management company Gluskin Sheff. "It assesses how confident the commercial banks are in lending to one another."

A narrow spread indicates confidence. A wide spread, less confidence. A really wide spread, pandemonium.

This matters because how much banks lend and what price they charge to borrow money has a major impact on the economy. Typically, more lending leads to economic growth. Less lending leads to a slowdown or even a recession.

"Invariably what happens in the financial arena ends up in the real side of the economy," Rosenberg says.

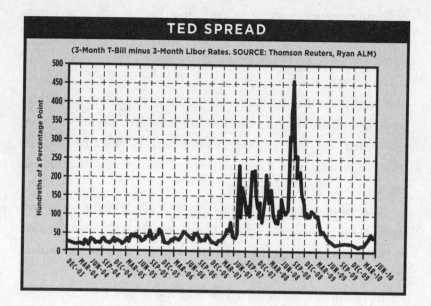

TED SPREAD

(3-Month T-Bill minus 3-Month Libor Rates. SOURCE: Thomson Reuters, Ryan ALM)

Investment Strategy

When the Ted Spread widens, the overall amount of lending in the economy contracts, and that ultimately leads to "a visible slowing in economic growth," explains Rosenberg. Likewise, when the Ted Spread narrows, it is a sign that lending is resuming. Or put another way, the appetite for taking on riskier loans by banks is increasing.

The Ted Spread widened in 1987, 1990, 1998, 2000, 2008, and 2010. Recessions did not follow in 1987 or 1998, but they did in 1990, 2000, and 2008.

So a rise in Ted clearly suggests that a period of slower

economic growth may be in the offing, but, as when interpreting other indicators, it's important to look for a sustained trend and corroborating evidence before acting.

In general, lower appetite for lending by banks is not auspicious for the economy, and it does change the risk-reward ratio in favor of making more cautious investment decisions.

"When you start noticing this indicator is widening, it's usually a sign to step to the sidelines and incrementally take risk off the table," says Rosenberg.

So look to invest in relatively low-risk assets like government or high-rated corporate bonds. If you want to stay in stocks, look at companies that specialize in consumer staples like manufacturers and retailers of soap, toothpaste, and shampoo.

But "don't do anything whole hog," he warns, meaning make changes to a portfolio of investments in small increments. And that's particularly pertinent given that the Ted Spread can narrow quickly, indicating that the banks once again feel better about lending.

EXEC SUMMARY: TED SPREAD

When to look: Continuously.

Where to look: You can calculate your own Ted Spread by looking up Libor rates and subtracting the T-bill rates. To be exact you need three-month T-bill rates and three-month Libor rates.

You can find both these rates in *The Wall Street Journal* online's "Market Data Center" at www.WSJMarkets.com. When you are there, you'll need to go to the "Bonds, Rates & Credit Markets" tab.

Alternatively, for U.S. Treasury yields, see the FRED database. For Libor, look at the website of the British Bankers' Association at www.bbalibor.com/bba.

What to watch for: Increases (decreases) in Ted spreads, the difference between Treasury yields and Libor.

What it means: Banks will be lending less (more) in the near future, slowing (stimulating) the economy.

What steps to take: Appropriate cyclical investment, i.e., lowering exposure incrementally to riskier assets like stocks as Ted spreads widen.

Risk level: Medium.

Profit possibility: $$

47

TEXAS "ZOMBIE BANK" RATIO
Leading

WHEN THE DEFINITIVE MOVIE of the Great Credit Crunch of 2008 is made, it should be given the subheading "Attack of the Killer Zombie Banks." Zombies, you may recall, are the undead, neither dead nor alive. Tortured by this unnatural state of being, they wreak havoc among the living until destroyed.

The zombie banks are similar. They cause havoc too. Neither alive enough to make loans, nor dead enough to die or get taken over, they linger and drag on the economy.

How do you know if your bank is a zombie bank? You use the so-called Texas Ratio. It was invented in the early 1980s by Gerard Cassidy and his colleagues at RBC Capital Markets.

In the simplest terms it compares the ratio of bad assets at a bank to its available capital. That available capital is a cushion against the firm going bust.

"I covered the Texas banks in the 1980s and what I learned from them was that when their Texas Ratio broke through 100% they went bust," says Cassidy, who's still with RBC Capital Markets—now in Portland, Maine—as a bank equity analyst. The simple reason that the 100% figure is so important is that at that point the bank's reserves or capital is wiped out by mounting bad debts.

The Texas Ratio can be a little tricky to calculate. The bad assets part, or numerator, contains the total book value of all nonperforming assets on the bank's books. That includes real estate the bank has repossessed (which sometimes goes by the moniker OREO, or other real estate owned) as well as loans that are in default or are being restructured. In short, it includes things that are going to cost the bank money, says Cassidy.

The denominator is the value of the bank's equity or book value, plus its reserves against loan losses. Intangible parts of the bank's equity, like goodwill, are excluded. The way to think about the denominator (the bank's tangible capital) is like the sandbags on the top of a riverbank that protect people living nearby from extraordinary floods, explains Cassidy.

Or in the parlance of finance, the bank's capital is the defense against bad loans wiping out everything. It's like the last line of defense against an attack of the undead. Banks with a higher level of bad debts and a high Texas Ratio are sometimes rescued by stronger banks. However, sometimes they just limp along like zombies.

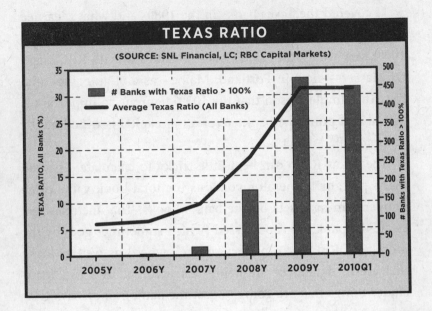

TEXAS RATIO

(SOURCE: SNL Financial, LC; RBC Capital Markets)

Investment Strategy

"A bank with a Texas Ratio over 100% is in dire straits," says Cassidy. "It's like driving a car with the tachometer in the red zone," he says. "If you keep doing that, eventually the car will blow up on you."

The biggest problem most people have when trying to use the Texas Ratio is that they forget to take out intangible equity—such as goodwill, trade secrets, copyrights, patents, and trademarks—from the denominator, says Cassidy. "When you see a bank having troubles, then goodwill and intangibles are usually worthless," he says.

EXEC SUMMARY: TEXAS "ZOMBIE BANK" RATIO

When to look: Daily.

Where to look: The Federal Deposit Insurance Corporation (FDIC) has the necessary data to calculate your own Texas Ratios for each bank at www.fdic.gov/bank/statistical/. Some data can also be gleaned from the Office of the Comptroller of the Currency at www.occ.treas.gov/pubinf.htm.

Alternatively, for banks that have publicly traded stock, an investor can glean information from the quarterly earnings release known as the 10Q, or the annual release known as the 10K.

What to watch for: Increases (decreases) in the Texas Ratio (nonperforming assets/tangible capital).

What it means: The bank or banking sector is more (less) likely to fail.

What steps to take: Sell (buy) the bank or sector especially as the ratio approaches the zombie land of 100%.

Risk level: Medium.

Profit possibility: $$

48

TIPS SPREAD
Leading

(See also PCE Deflator, Real Interest Rate)

T HE WORDS OF WALL Street forecasters are often cheap. So
when you really want to know what people are thinking
about the future you should watch what they *do*, not what they *say*.

More specifically, by looking at the actions of investors in
two different parts of the U.S. government bond market, we can
calculate expectations of future inflation. We derive the answer
not by what people say, but rather by how much the average investor is willing to pay for the bonds in question.

The two types of bonds to compare are government-issued
inflation-indexed securities, commonly known as TIPS, and
standard term debt sold by the U.S. Treasury. TIPS stands for
Treasury Inflation Protected Securities, a type of bond that
compensates investors when inflation increases. With regular

bonds, by contrast, holders are hurt as inflation rises because the purchasing power of the nominally fixed interest payments and the principal declines over time.

Treasuries typically offer a higher nominal interest rate than TIPS do. In other words, they promise to pay more dollars of interest per one hundred dollars invested. But the actual interest payment of the TIPS is adjusted in the future for the effects of inflation. The difference between the yields of the two types of securities is the expected future rate of inflation at that point in time. It's known as the TIPS spread, or the TIPS breakeven.

Here's an example: If ten-year Treasuries are yielding 4% and TIPS 1%, then the future inflation rate is expected to be 3% a year for the next ten years. The difference, or spread, between the yields changes every day based on changes in the prices of the two types of bond.

Investors tend to put a lot of weight on this metric because it gives them an insight into bond market investors' inflation expectations. Unlike in some markets, trading in government bonds is almost entirely carried out by sophisticated investors who tend to act rationally. (That's quite unlike the stock market, which has a sizable portion of retail investors who have acted quite irrationally at times.)

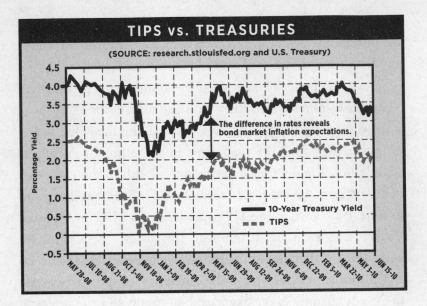

TIPS vs. TREASURIES
(SOURCE: research.stlouisfed.org and U.S. Treasury)

The difference in rates reveals bond market inflation expectations.

10-Year Treasury Yield

TIPS

Investment Strategy

The TIPS spread matters because it tells you what level of inflation a very savvy part of the market is expecting.

Expectations are key with inflation because they can be self-fulfilling. If you and everyone around you think prices of goods and services are going to rise, then prices have a worrisome tendency to do so. Because of this self-fulfilling problem with inflation expectations, the Fed keeps a close eye on this part of the bond market.

Accordingly, we can also get a read on when the Federal Reserve might change the cost of borrowing, explains bond market veteran and head of New Jersey–based research outfit Marta on the Markets, T. J. Marta. "Two percent seems to be the dividing line between hiking and easing," explains Marta. What he means is that when inflation expectations are above 2% a year, the Fed will likely raise the cost of borrowing. In this case, long-term bonds may be in for a rally, he says. "That is seen as the Fed bringing inflation under control and so yields come down [and prices of bonds go up]," he says.

When expectations are for inflation lower than 2% a year, the Fed will likely not raise short-term interest rates. As a result, the short-term cost of borrowing will stay low and that tends to be good for commodities, explains Marta. He also says equities can do well in that scenario too.

Marta points out, however, that the TIPS spread sometimes temporarily jumps above 2%, so, as with all indicators, it's important to see that a sustainable trend develops before leaping into action.

EXEC SUMMARY: TIPS SPREAD

When to look: Daily.

Where to look: Data on TIPS yields and Treasury yields are available in *The Wall Street Journal* online's "Market Data Center" at www.WSJMarkets.com. When you are there, you'll need to go to the "Bonds, Rates & Credit Markets" section.

Alternatively, the FRED database has yields on both TIPS and regular Treasuries. The U.S. Treasury's website, www.treasury direct.gov/, also has information on TIPS.

What to watch for: Sustained inflation expectations greater than (less than) 2% as measured by the TIPS spread.

What it means: The Fed will likely raise (not raise) interest rates.

What steps to take: Appropriate cyclical investments. For example, when the TIPS spread points to monetary policy tightening by the Fed, consider buying less risky assets, like high grade corporate bonds, and selling riskier ones, like stocks.

Risk level: Medium.

Profit possibility: $$$

49

CBOE VOLATILITY INDEX (VIX)
Leading

D OGS, THEY SAY, CAN smell fear. Well, you can too, in an
entirely objective manner. That's important because fear
and greed are what drive the action on Wall Street. While we
can't measure greed very well—it's just too subjective—we can
easily measure fear.

It's done using the VIX, or the CBOE Volatility Index: The
higher the VIX, the greater the level of anxiety among investors. If ever there was a "tell" on Wall Street, this is it.

In the simplest terms, the VIX measures the cost to buy
protection against the broad stock market falling. The more
investors are willing to pay for this "insurance," the more anx-
ious they are overall. So while it still won't let you see through
the tough emotional shell of an investment banker, it will give
you an idea of how scared they are as a group.

The VIX is a relative measure of the cost of buying options on the S&P 500 Index, the most popular broad measure of the U.S. stock market. Traded on the Chicago Board Options Exchange, these options[5] act like insurance protection from unforeseen stock market crashes like in 1929, 1987, or 2008. The more uncertain investors feel about future events, the more they are willing to pay for that insurance, so they bid up the price of the options.

The theoretical value of options is most frequently determined using the Black-Scholes formula, named after the two canny economists who invented it in the 1970s. The formula uses a number of different inputs, including interest rates, length of the option contract, the relative prices of the index, and last but not least, volatility. The key thing to know is that at any point in time every variable except volatility is already determined. Traders look at the market price of the option and solve for the volatility variable. They call the result "implied volatility." That's precisely what the VIX is: implied volatility.

---

[5] Options are fixed-term contracts that give the purchaser of the contract the right to buy (or sell, depending on the contract) the index at a predetermined price. Profits or losses are made from the difference between the contract price and the market price of the index at the expiration of the option contract.

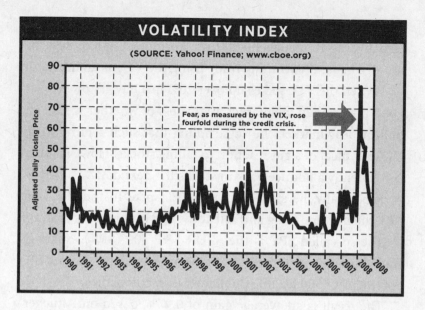

VOLATILITY INDEX

(SOURCE: Yahoo! Finance; www.cboe.org)

Fear, as measured by the VIX, rose fourfold during the credit crisis.

Investment Strategy

Someone else's fear can help you make money on Wall Street. But first you need to avoid some highly risky strategies.

Most notably, some investors use changes in the level of the VIX to buy or sell options. That may work for them, but before you try it, consider this: "Buying options is a way to lose lots of money really, really quickly." That's what one veteran investor advised one of the authors. This is especially so for the novice investor, so if that's you, avoid options.

Of course that doesn't mean the VIX is useless. On top of just a general sense of collective anxiety on Wall Street, there are ways to snag some profits.

James Altucher, managing director of New York–based alternative asset management firm Formula Capital, says he's found a generally winning trade using the VIX as an indicator.

"When the VIX spikes up over 20% in a day, it's often a very good time to buy the market, regardless of whether we are in a bull or bear market," he says, noting that such a jump in the VIX is typical of a gut reaction to falling stocks. However, there is frequently a bounce back in stocks the next day.

Specifically, he says, after the 20% spike in the VIX "buy SPY the next morning and sell at the end of that day's trading."

The so-called SPY is the SPDR S&P 500 (SPY) exchange-traded fund, which tracks the value of the widely followed S&P 500 Index of 500 leading publicly traded companies.

The result is an average gain of 0.97%, based on Altucher's analysis of data going back to 1993 through mid-2010. The 20%-plus jump in the VIX happened only thirty times, but the suggested trade would have been profitable in twenty-two cases or 73% of the time.

The average return of nearly 1% is "enormous" for a one-day trade, says Altucher. It's roughly equivalent to over 200% in annualized returns. He notes that transactions costs, at about one cent a share, are minimal with this trade, and that the days when the trade didn't win saw only modest losses.

"In the past seventeen years, doing the system described above but holding for a month instead of a day would've resulted in an average return of –0.64% per trade," he says, noting the worst year was 2008. Excluding the data from 2008, the monthlong trade would have seen profits on average.

EXEC SUMMARY: CBOE VOLATILITY INDEX (VIX)

When to look: Continuously.

Where to look: Data on the VIX is available at the main page of *The Wall Street Journal* online's "Market Data Center" at www.WSJMarkets.com. When you are there, look for "CBOE Volatility VIX."

Alternatively, data on the VIX can be found at Yahoo! Finance at www.finance.yahoo.com and the Chicago Board Options Exchange at www.cboe.org.

What to watch for: An upward daily spike in the VIX of 20% or more.

What it means: There may be excess fear in the market, making it ripe for a bounce.

What steps to take: Buy a broad market ETF like SPY the morning after the spike and sell it at the end of that same day.

Risk level: Astronomical.

Profit possibility: $$$$

50

VIXEN INDEX
Coincident

THE VIXEN IS OTHERWISE known as the Hot Waitress Index. The idea is that when the waitresses at your local eateries and bars look smoking hot, then it's a surefire guarantee that the economy is in the doldrums.

This indicator first came to light in 2009 in the depths of the economic crisis when Hugo Lindgren, then editorial director for *New York* magazine, wrote a piece about it for his magazine. Apparently this wasn't just a desperate attempt to "fill space" inside the advert-heavy glossy publication.

Believe it or not, there is some serious economic theory behind this index, and it all relates to employment opportunities.

"There're a whole lot of businesses that are interested in hiring attractive people," says Lindgren. "That's true for both men and women."

But Lindgren points out that beautiful women are valued

more by businesses than attractive men. That's why this is called the Vixen, and not the Stud, indicator.

In general, employers—particularly those in the service economy—generally place a premium on good-looking people. That's not just in runway modeling, but also for all manner of social/commercial events. A company in New York called BarCandy, for example, specializes in providing attractive bartenders for fancy events.

When the economy booms, "beautiful people" snag these better-paid gigs. They don't tend to work at the local greasy spoon. But as things get rough in the economy and the well-paid jobs dry up, they may take the regular restaurant positions.

So next time you notice that the waitstaff at your local diner is drop-dead gorgeous, then you can rightfully suspect that the economy is in crisis mode. Either that or you are living in Los Angeles.

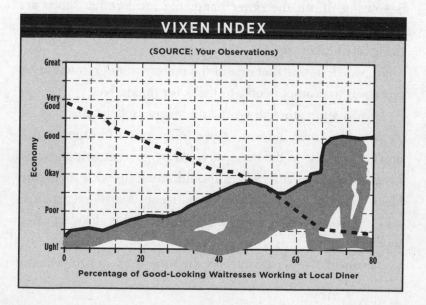

VIXEN INDEX

(SOURCE: Your Observations)

Economy (vertical axis): Great, Very Good, Good, Okay, Poor, Ugh!

Percentage of Good-Looking Waitresses Working at Local Diner (horizontal axis): 0, 20, 40, 60, 80

Investment Strategy

It's a little tricky to apply this indicator. That's because your view of what is attractive is unlikely to be exactly the same as anyone else's. For that reason you have to collect your data yourself, not from others. And you should try to ensure that you are in the same state of mind each time.

To get an accurate read on this indicator some serious study is in order. Yep, your homework assignment is to check out the waitstaff at your local eatery. One trip will not suffice.

You'll need to take notes and to do so each time you visit the eatery because the key to this indicator is establishing a trend. It is not really about the absolute level of cuteness.

For instance, is the beauty of the waitresses improving over time? If it is, then perhaps that marks a sign that the economy is souring. If, on the other hand, the local coffee shops are staffed by the hideous and unattractive, then you can be sure things are looking up.

It's worth noting that one of the reasons Lindgren wrote his piece was to prompt people to think for themselves.

"It was a fun story to write as a means to help others come up with their own indexes," says Lindgren. Or in other words, don't rely solely on the data provided by government agencies. Instead would-be forecasters should come up with their own ideas. Former Federal Reserve chairman Alan Greenspan is said to favor watching scrap metal prices and underwear sales, says Lindgren.

Meanwhile, other people say the time it takes you to hail a

cab on a New York City street is a fair indication of how strapped consumers are feeling. The "taxi indicator" has a lot of merit. That's because the number of cabs on the street is basically fixed. What isn't fixed is the demand for those cabs. The spending on taxis waxes and wanes with the relative strength of the economy.

As people hail more cabs, there are less free ones available for you so it takes you longer to catch one. In short, if you can consistently get a cab instantly at rush hour in Midtown Manhattan, then the economy must suck. Likewise, if you can't get one easily even in the off-peak hours, then things must be looking up. And if you run into a string of attractive cabbies, head for the hills!

EXEC SUMMARY: VIXEN INDEX

When to look: Whenever you visit a restaurant.

Where to look: Because *The Wall Street Journal* is a family publication you won't find too many hot waitresses in its pages. That means you are kind of on your own with this indicator. But if you have read this far in this book, you are well on your way to being able to act on your own. You might be reading this in a coffee shop right now. If so, make note of the attractiveness of the staff. Write it down (maybe even on this page) along with the location and the date and then do the same again and again and again. Pretty soon you'll have enough data to work with.

But more than just developing the Vixen, do as Hugo Lindgren suggests and think of your own indicators. Try them out. If they work, keep using them. If not, discard them. But most of all have fun and never, ever make big money decisions on the basis of any one indicator, no matter how attractive it may seem.

What to watch for: An increase in the attractiveness of local waitstaff.

What it means: Well-paid jobs where beauty is required are scarce. The economy is softer than the pudding you just ordered.

What steps to take: Ask the hot waitress out, then buy defensive stocks like utilities, food retailers, and pharmaceutical companies.

Risk level: Astronomical.

Profit possibility: $$$$

CONCLUSION

Putting It All Together

I F YOU'VE READ AND then reread our Fantastic 50, you are now in a position to start putting it all together. As you do that, remember that economic forecasting is more art than science. Far more!

Here are a few tips, in no particular order:

First, be more than a little wary of mathematical models because they give a false sense of precision and hence security. Saying the economy will grow 2.3422674% next year is an absurd statement. Be wary of anyone who says otherwise.

Likewise, numbers from official sources can give a false sense of accuracy. When the government says the unemployment rate is 9.6%, remember that it is an estimated figure based on a small sample of households. Better to say it's broadly 10%. Better still to note whether it's falling or rising month to month. That's far more telling.

Instead of looking for exactness in numbers, look to gain experience and improve judgment by understanding some basic models of economic causation. They are far superior, and far more flexible than just figures. We outlined some basic ideas in the individual economic chapters of the Fantastic 50.

Still, while you look at those models, remember that forecasting is a moving target. Statistical relationships between variables that held last decade, last year, or even last week may no longer ring true. That is why data immersion, though it will strike many as redundant, is so important. And that is also why we packed multiple indicators into the sections covering the different parts of the economy (with one exception: the government, where we felt one was sufficient).

After all, consider this: Say X, Y, and Z all traditionally move in lockstep and typically precede A. You might conclude that you can just track X and forget about Y and Z. But then you'll miss a structural change in the economic beast that makes Y alone presage A while X and Z head off in the opposite direction.

An investor in tune with all three series, by contrast, will note the anomaly and tread cautiously. That way you don't lose your shirt. Former Federal Reserve chairman Alan Greenspan was an advocate of immersion, poring over reams and reams of data before making the predictions upon which he based U.S. monetary policy. He didn't always get it right but he had a far better record than most!

As information flows faster, there are pressures to forecast ever more quickly and accurately. If you are feeling that pressure, you may be tempted to concentrate on a few broad indicators rather than the fifty we specify. Don't!

Why? Because doing so will give you major problems. The broader an economic indicator is, the less accurate it is. Or put another way, metrics that look at overall economic activity tend to be crude at measuring. That insight is just an application of the risk-return tradeoff well known to investors. A quick read of indicators used to make investment decisions sometimes may work but often will backfire.

At the other extreme, you could wait until the NBER completes its extensive (but backward-looking) evaluation of many different measures of the economy that define when the business cycle starts and finishes. The problem with doing so: You'll miss the boat every time. That's because by the time NBER calls a recession or expansion the actual event is long gone—so long gone that it's almost a historical event! By that time the relevant investment opportunities are history too.

What you need to do is look at a variety of indicators that cover all the areas of the economy and learn to make decisions on investments while there is still some uncertainty. Indeed, you may be ahead of the pack compared to those who haven't studied the Fantastic 50 and may hear from friends that the economy is great when you see multiple signs that it's heading for a slump. Learn through experience to trust your judgment.

Choosing Indicators Wisely

Before using any indicator, it is crucially important to understand the difference between cyclical and structural changes. Cyclical is what happens during the business cycle—recession followed by expansion and then recession again. Structural changes happen when things fundamentally change in the economy, like the advent of the automobile in the early twentieth century.

A recent example happened in the United Kingdom. The number of items mailed in Britain was long an economic indicator. When the economy grew briskly, there was more need to use the post for advertising, magazine subscriptions, contracts, checks, etc., so the Royal Mail's volume increased commensurately. Starting around 1999–2000, however, use of the mail service dropped even while Britain's economy expanded. During the Great Recession, the volume of letters dropped many times faster than the rate of economic activity. To use the Royal Mail's decline as an indicator of the imminent demise of the British economy was false. The steep decline in postal volume has more to do with technology (e-mail, websites, electronic signatures, etc.) than with the level of economic activity in Britain.

Similarly, as we mentioned earlier in the book, investors once believed that what was good for General Motors was good for America, and vice versa. If GM's earnings were poor, they'd take that as a sign of an economic downturn. That might have made sense in the 1950s. But over time the correlation between GM's fortunes and those of the nation have grown weaker. Today, an investor might even see sagging GM sales as a sign of a stronger economy to come, if only the government would let the once-behemoth company fail, thus allowing hundreds of more innovative companies to spring forth from the nutrients (engineers, robots, unused factories, etc.) provided by its giant, rotting corpse. At the time of this writing, GM was partially government owned, following a massive bailout. That's something the authors think never should have happened.

Some forecasters use the number of patents granted annually as a measure of economic activity. But it's tricky to use that figure because it may be both a coincident indicator (that dutifully fell during the Great Depression and the 1970s) and a farsighted leading indicator that measures future productivity growth. Patents granted today, in other words, will allow us to produce more tomorrow. People spend good time and money inventing stuff and protecting it with a patent, so they must expect it to be valuable. Right? Right!

However, in many places, including the United States, obtaining and maintaining a patent is pretty cheap in the scheme of things. So, while we might stipulate that all patents have positive expected value (expected profits exceed the costs of patenting), all patents are not equally important. The difference in economic impact, both in profits and in spillover effects, between the first computer chip and the first holy water dispenser, for example, was undoubtedly huge. But it's hard to tell how much more. Quality matters here big time, in other words, but it's tricky to measure ahead of time.

Even more troubling, the number of patents granted is far from a clean measure due to changes in patent office rules and efficiency. Some, most, or even all of the apparent falloff in patenting activity in the 1970s, for example, was due to a smaller percentage of patent applications being accepted and a long backlog of cases awaiting review due to government staff cuts.

Another classic error in forecasting is to simply go by the idea that if an expansion or a recession lasts longer than average, then a turning point is imminent. There is no reason why a recession can't last half a century— just ask somebody from Cuba or North Korea—and no reason why an expansion can't last much longer than "average," which of course will be highly sensitive to start and end dates. According to the NBER, for example, the average expansion since 1854 has been thirty-eight months, yet seven expansions since then have lasted fifty or more months, i.e., a full year or more past the average date.

Investors also need to be careful that they don't read too much into complex indicators like the number of Mexicans coming illegally to the United States for work (even if that figure is possible to measure). As the Comedy Central TV cartoon series *South Park* showed brilliantly in its 2004 episode "Goobacks," the level of Mexican immigration is a function of the *relative* health of the Mexican and U.S. economies, not solely a barometer of the American economy. So while the estimated number of immigrants in 2009 was well off its peak of over 1.5 million in 2000, immigration actually began to slide in 2005–6, well before the Great Recession. It was not that potential Mexican immigrants were particularly prescient and foresaw the financial crisis; it was that the Mexican economy improved vis-à-vis the U.S. economy at that time and continued to do so through 2009.

The financial markets are forward looking, so investors need to be too. The early bird doesn't necessarily get the worm as it might miss hours of sleep only to arrive in the wrong, wormless place. Like above-market returns, worms are elusive creatures that do not often appear in the same place twice, at least on successive days, so it is the smart bird, the predictive one, that will get the worm and do so with minimal cost. Likewise for investors, you must be somewhat anticipatory in order to profit.

Our Magic Bullets

In addition to telling you a little about the Fantastic 50 indicators, we have tried to establish the following points:

- Successful investing means making and *keeping* above-market returns at each stage of the business cycle.

- Investors must correctly forecast the business cycle before they can know which types of specific investments (bonds, equities, commodities, real estate) are likely to generate superior returns.

- Investing is not a one-off event. It is a learning process, a lifetime commitment to understanding the economy in all its glorious complexity.

- Forecasting, like investment more generally, is more art than science. Correct reasoning and big-picture prescience trump quantitative and mathematical precision based on dubious assumptions.

Conclusion

- Your capacity to accurately predict stems from a combination of sound historical trend data and a model that correctly identifies causal agents rather than mere statistical correlations.

- Economic indicators may lead, coincide with, or lag actual economic conditions, as measured by per capita output or GDP, which is the sum of consumption, investment, government expenditures, and net exports $(C + I + G + NX)$.

- The more indicators an investor tracks, the better feel for the economy she will develop and the more confident she can be that changes in the business cycle are in the offing.

- The fifty indicators described in this book are the best because they are the most timely, accurate, and relevant to the real economy and also relatively unknown.

- While lagging and coincident indicators are important to follow in order to understand the economy in all its complexity, leading indicators are the most important to investors.

- Occasionally, though, the component pieces of a coincident indicator are timely and provide a glimpse of the future and can therefore be as useful as leading indicators.

Reading a book explaining these economic indicators—and how you can profit using them—once is one thing. Actually applying it is quite another. So how do you put this knowledge into practice?

What you need is a plan to really master the material. First, start by setting aside a period each day to study just a couple of the indicators. The best way to choose which ones to study and when is to mark a calendar when each new set of data on each indicator is coming out. Most of the indicators have specific and predictable release dates and times. Current release dates are listed in our Exec Summaries. *The Wall Street Journal* has a calendar online: http://online.wsj.com/mdc/public/page/2_3063 -economicCalendar.html?mod=topnav_2_3000. Also, Briefing. com maintains a calendar of economic data release dates and times at www.briefing.com/Investor/Public/Calendars/Economic Calendar.htm.

Because most data comes out in the morning New York time, we suggest dedicating some time the evening before it is to be released to reread the chapter on the indicator(s) in question. When you've read and reread the chapter, also read the financial press. There are frequently articles that outline what investors are expecting from the new data and what it might mean if various scenarios occur.

In the morning get up early to see what the data says. Also at that time it will pay off to read what the financial press actually says about the new data. Most days of the month (there are twenty-two workdays in an average month) have some economic data reported. So you could set up a study calendar around that schedule.

That said, some of the indicators we featured are privately published (e.g., the Credit Availability Oscillator) or don't have regular release dates (VIX, Vixen, Texas Ratio, etc.). This makes life a tad trickier. But this is where your regular perusal of the business press will pay back. You'll develop ways to find the information you need to follow those indicators. Whenever you come across the information you need for these nonpublic or qualitative indicators reread the relevant chapters.

Follow that study schedule of reading the chapter the night before and then analyzing the actual data the next day for at least two months. At that time you may be ready to start keeping an investing diary.

This is where you make "paper trades." In other words, you "buy and sell" assets based on what you are learning about the economy. But here's the key: The trades are only on paper. No actual money should be used at this stage. The idea here is to try out the knowledge you are learning but in a safe and cost-free way. For ease of calculation, use closing prices of the securities or assets you "buy" and "sell" for your phantom "account."

Use this paper account for at least six months, possibly longer. When you feel ready, start making investments with real money. At first you should be cautious because you will undoubtedly still make mistakes. However, by using the knowledge you've gained in this book and in your studies, these investing missteps will hopefully be fewer and less damaging than before. And that can lead to something all investors are looking for: bigger profits and less stress.

APPENDIX

Useful Economic Indicators Websites

GENERAL

Briefing.com: www.briefing.com has a free "Investor" section and an economic calendar.

CONSUMPTION

Bureau of Labor Statistics: www.BLS.gov has a plethora of information about unemployment, efficiency, and the makeup of the U.S. workforce, as well as producer prices and lots of other data.

Bureau of Transportation: www.bts.gov/publications/national_transportation_statistics/Statistics has details of car sales.

Conference Board: www.conference-board.org provides details on consumer sentiment.

Redbook Research and Chain Store Age: www.chainstoreage.com/indus

trydata/monthlysales.aspx?menuid=471 and www.redbookresearch
.com have data on retail sales.

INVESTMENT

Economic Cycle Research Institute (ECRI): www.businesscycle.com has
data on the WLI and the JoC-ECRI IPI, plus other indices and metrics.

Institute for Supply Management: www.ism.ws has data on the ISM Manufacturing Survey as well as the ISM Non-Manufacturing Survey.

Kitco: www.Kitco.com, www.kitcometals.com, www.kitcosilver.com provide deep resources for metals market watchers.

London Metal Exchange: www.lme.co.uk has details of base metals prices
as well as regular reporting on metals inventories.

National Association of Realtors: www.realtor.org has a slew of data available on the housing market.

New York Mercantile Exchange (part of the CME Group): www.cmegroup
.com provides data on energy and metals.

Semiconductor Industry Association: www.SIA.org has details of the
book-to-bill ratio.

World Bureau of Metals Statistics: www.world-bureau.com has details of
the global metals markets.

GOVERNMENT

U.S. Treasury: www.treasury.gov has loads of information on the economy
and taxes.

White House: www.whitehouse.gov publishes data on the government.

NET EXPORTS

Baltic Exchange: www.balticexchange.com for the oceangoing freight rates.

Bank of Japan: www.boj.or.jp/en/ for the Tankan Survey and other Japan-specific data.

Central Intelligence Agency: www.cia.gov has basic economic data on most countries.

Economist: www.economist.com provides details on the Big Mac Index and other economic data.

Energy Information Administration: www.eia.gov provides details on oil inventories.

International Monetary Fund: www.imf.org has information on almost all countries in the world.

Organization of Economic Cooperation and Development: www.oecd.org has data on the world's rich countries.

World Bank: www.worldbank.org has data on over 1,200 economic indicators, from agriculture to education and the environment to health, for over two hundred nations.

MULTIPLE COMPONENTS

British Bankers' Association: www.bbalibor.com for Libor quotes.

Bureau of Economic Analysis: www.bea.gov maintains data on income, spending, and savings as well as many other data.

Census Bureau: www.census.gov has information on durable goods orders, the housing market, and numerous other economic indicators.

Centers for Disease Control: www.cdc.gov provides demographic data.

Federal Reserve: www.federalreserve.gov has data and research reports on a slew of things including industrial production, as well as the famed Beige Book.

Daily Finance: www.dailyfinance.com has data on short interest.

FRED database at the St. Louis Fed: http://research.stlouisfed.org/fred2/ provides time series data on over two thousand national economic variables, including banking, business, prices, employment, exchange rates, output, interest rates, monetary aggregates, and international transactions.

Office of the Comptroller of the Currency: www.occ.gov/pubinf.htm has the data for analyzing banks.

Philadelphia Fed: www.phil.frb.org has data on the Aruoba-Diebold-Scotti Business Conditions Index and its Business Outlook Survey.

The Wall Street Journal: www.wsj.com has masses of news and analysis plus a handy-dandy data center.

Yahoo! Finance: finance.yahoo.com has time series data on stocks, indices, and exchange-traded funds.

INFLATION, FEAR, AND UNCERTAINTY

Chicago Board Options Exchange: www.cboe.org has data on the VIX.

Federal Deposit Insurance Corporation (FDIC): www.fdic.gov/bank/statistical/ has data needed to calculate the Texas Ratio.

London Bullion Market Association: lbma.org.uk has historical data on gold and silver prices.

Misery Index: www.miseryindex.us has data on inflation and unemployment that it combines into the Misery Index.

SELECTED BIBLIOGRAPHY

Axilrod, Stephen. *Inside the Fed: Monetary Policy and Its Management, Martin through Greenspan to Bernanke*. Cambridge: MIT Press, 2009.

Baumohl, Bernard. *The Secrets of Economic Indicators: Hidden Clues to Future Economic Trends and Investment Opportunities*, 2nd ed. Philadelphia: Wharton School Publishing, 2008.

Birchenhall, Chris, Hans Jessen, Denise Osborn, and Paul Simpson. "Predicting U.S. Business-Cycle Regimes," *Journal of Business and Economic Statistics* 17 (July 1999): 313–23.

Boldin, Michael. "Dating Turning Points in Economic Cycles," *Journal of Business* 67 (January 1994): 97–131.

Bordo, Michael. "The Limits of Economic Forecasting," *Cato Journal* 12 (Spring/Summer 1992): 44–48.

Fleckenstein, William A. and Frederick Sheehan. *Greenspan's Bubbles: The Age of Ignorance at the Federal Reserve*. New York: McGraw Hill, 2008.

Friedman, Walter. "The Harvard Economic Service and the Problems of Forecasting," *History of Political Economy* 41 (2009): 57–88.

Griliches, Zvi. "Patent Statistics as Economic Indicators: A Survey," *Journal of Economic Literature* 28 (December 1990): 1661–707.

Kaufman, Henry. *On Money and Markets: A Wall Street Memoir*. New York: McGraw Hill, 2000.

McCloskey, Deirdre. "The Art of Forecasting: From Ancient to Modern Times," *Cato Journal* 12 (Spring/Summer 1992): 23–43.

Rogers, R. Mark. *The Complete Idiot's Guide to Economic Indicators*. New York: Alpha, 2009.

Stock, James and Mark Watson. "New Indexes of Coincident and Leading Economic Indicators," *NBER Macroeconomics Annual* 4 (1989): 351–94.

Wright, Robert E. *Fubarnomics: A Lighthearted, Serious Look at America's Economic Ills*. Buffalo: Prometheus, 2010.

Wright, Robert E. and Vincenzo Quadrini. *Money and Banking*. Irvington, N.Y.: Flat World Knowledge: 2009. www.flatworld knowledge.com/printed-book/1634.

ACKNOWLEDGMENTS

No book can be completed or even attempted without the help of many others. In addition to all the people quoted in this book, there were many, many others.

In particular, we both highlight Roe D'Angelo and Matt Inman for their patience and perseverance during the editing process. We never said we were easy!

In addition, Mr. Constable says thanks dearly to Courtney Lutterman without whose moral support this would not have been possible. Thanks are also due to Alan Murray and Rick Stine for making a whole host of things possible at Dow Jones. Others notable for their encouragement in this project include Neal Lipschutz, Brett Arends, Julie Iannuzzi, Shawn Bender, Bob Bruner, and Ken Eades.

Dr. Wright thanks David Backus, Michael Darda, Jan Reid, Mark Stickle, and Richard Sylla. Finally, we apologize in advance for any omissions. You know who you are even if we forgot to mention you!

BOOKS FROM
THE WALL STREET JOURNAL

THE WALL STREET JOURNAL GUIDE TO THE 50 ECONOMIC INDICATORS THAT REALLY MATTER

From Big Macs to "Zombie Banks," the Indicators Smart Investors Watch to Beat the Market

By Simon Constable and Robert E. Wright

ISBN 978-0-06-200138-2 (paperback)

The smart new must-have guide from *The Wall Street Journal* includes 4-page descriptions of 50 economic indicators, the data that economists use to predict changes in the economy's direction and that investors use to make savvy decisions.

THE WALL STREET JOURNAL GUIDE TO INVESTING IN THE APOCALYPSE

Make Money by Seeing Opportunity Where Others See Peril

By James Altucher & Douglas R. Sease

ISBN 978-0-06-200132-0 (paperback)

This essential guide advises savvy investors on how to anticipate and prepare for seemingly earth-shattering events—how to measure the risks and adjust their investments—to gain a substantial advantage in reaping profits while others are frozen with fear.

THE WALL STREET JOURNAL GUIDE TO THE NEW RULES OF PERSONAL FINANCE

The Essential Strategies for Saving, Investing, and Building a Portfolio in a World Turned Upside Down

By Dave Kansas

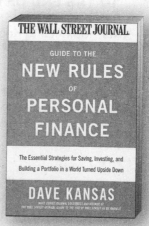

ISBN 978-0-06-198632-1 (paperback)

In this definitive guide to the new world of personal finance, Dave Kansas takes everything you thought you knew about saving, managing risk, and constructing a portfolio and turns it upside down. Incorporating old ideas that still work with new strategies and tactics, this book helps investors take advantage of the radically new financial world.

THE WALL STREET JOURNAL ESSENTIAL GUIDE TO MANAGEMENT

Lasting Lessons from the Best Leadership Minds of Our Time

By Alan Murray

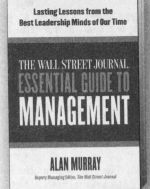

ISBN 978-0-06-184033-3 (paperback)
The definitive guide on how to be a successful manager at any level, across all kinds of industries and organizations, from the deputy managing editor of *The Wall Street Journal*.

THE WALL STREET JOURNAL GUIDE TO POWER TRAVEL

How to Arrive with Your Dignity, Sanity, and Wallet Intact

By Scott McCartney

ISBN 978-0-06-168871-3 (paperback)
Imagine a world without late planes, missed connections, lost luggage, bumped passengers, cramped seating, high fares, and security lines. From *The Wall Street Journal* "Middle Seat" columnist, this book shows readers how to secure ease, civility, comfort, and good deals on the road.

THE WALL STREET JOURNAL GUIDE TO THE END OF WALL STREET AS WE KNOW IT

What You Need to Know About the Greatest Financial Crisis of Our Time— and How to Survive It

By Dave Kansas

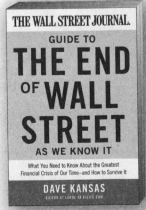

ISBN 978-0-06-178840-6 (paperback)
The definitive resource for Main Street readers who want to make sense of what's happening on Wall Street, better understand how we got here, and what we need to know in the days to come.